NEW DIRECTIONS FOR THE RURAL CHURCH

NEW DIRECTIONS
FOR THE RURAL CHURCH

Case Studies in Area Ministry

by
David M. Byers
and
Bernard Quinn

PAULIST PRESS
New York/Ramsey/Toronto

Library of Congress
Catalog Card Number: 77-14799

ISBN: 0-8091-2085-2

Published by Paulist Press
Editorial Office: 1865 Broadway, New York, N.Y. 10023
Business Office: 545 Island Road, Ramsey, N.J. 07446

Printed and bound in the
United States of America

Contents

Preface

This past decade has witnessed the emergence of many new organizations for Christian ministry structured at a level between parish and diocese. Some of these organizations operate apostolic programs, some are advisory bodies and still others provide support to church leaders in their lives and work. They may range in size and complexity from a committee set up by two parishes to direct a single joint program to an elaborately-structured council operating in 20 counties. But they all serve the Church's mission in what we have chosen to call an "area"—a territory larger than a parish and smaller than a diocese.

This book offers an introduction to the growing phenomenon of area ministry. The topic has been restricted in two ways. Although area ministry organizations have flourished in both metropolitan and nonmetropolitan settings, we are concerned only with those which operate largely in rural America. Second, our investigation covers only Catholic groups and ecumenical groups in which there is significant Catholic participation. Because of these limitations, we make no attempt to generalize about area ministry in all its forms.

Since the book deals with new and unfamiliar developments in ministry, we have tried to give the reader a glimpse of the living reality rather than relying on abstract analysis. Chapters 2 through 9 are case studies of eight organizations engaged in area ministry from New York State to Texas. Each of these chapters contains some evaluative comments. But the case studies are not evaluations in the strict sense, just as the organizations themselves are not controlled experiments. The emphasis is on telling a story rather than on making a judgment.

The fact that these eight organizations have been chosen for inclusion in the book will create a presumption that they are uniquely successful. Certainly, none of them is a failure; we have included no negative examples. Neither should they be regarded as models for imitation, however. These particular groups were selected because they represent a wide range of area ministries and because they concretize the ongoing struggle toward a better rural apostolate.

The case studies are the product of a survey of over 100 area organizations which the Glenmary Research Center conducted early in 1975. This survey also forms the background for the outline of rural area ministry given in Chapter 1. Here we define terms, describe the needs to which area ministry responds, sketch the changing socioeconomic context in which it has developed and provide a classification system which sorts out its three principal types. We hope that those contemplating new area organizations or involved in existing ones will find this overview helpful for planning and reflection. As a further aid to the interpretation of the case studies, we have added two appendices. The first is a list of key definitions arranged in schematic form. The second is a transcription of the constitutions or guidelines by which five of the eight organizations operate.

The two authors, who form the professional staff of the Glenmary Research Center in Washington, D.C., are jointly responsible for everything in this volume. Without the cooperation of many minds and hands, however, it could never have been written. We owe a special debt of gratitude to the following: Rev. J. Kendrick Williams of the Town and Country Apostolic Council; Rev. Robert Johnson of the Northeast Texas Clergy-Religious Group; Rev. Donald Brooks of Deanery Three Council; Rev. John Bush, Rev. Lawrence Gill, Rev. William Krudwig and Rev. Eugene Moll of the Interchurch Coordinating Council; Rev. Paul Connelly, Rev. Lawrence Hoffman and Rev. Joseph McDonnell of the Leon Regional Catholic Community; Mr. James Romer and Rev. Robert Butziger of the Morgan-Scott Project; Rev. Douglas Hoffman of the Diocese of Rochester; and Dr. E. W. Mueller and Rev. Victor Pavlenko of the Center for Community Organization and Area Development.

1. Area Ministry

Looked at from one angle, there is nothing new about area ministry. It has a long and honorable history. Diocesan high schools are area ministry organizations. So are most church-related hospitals, local offices of diocesan agencies and a growing number of deaneries. One cannot even claim that it is new to the rural Church; on the contrary, the Methodist circuit rider of frontier days was an area worker. Quietly, without creating much stir, area ministry organizations have long since become a feature of the settled landscape of American religion.

And yet, area ministry is undeniably new. The term itself is an invention, coined for the purpose of discussing church structures that operate on a level between parish and diocese. (The term "regional" was considered and rejected; it usually designates a territory larger than most dioceses, as in the "Appalachian Region" or the "Great Lakes Region.") The fact that a significant number of area ministry groups are ecumenical is a product of very recent history. Finally, many of the forms which modern area organizations have adopted and some of the tasks they perform are experimental. In response to changed conditions both within and outside the Church, area ministry has blossomed in the past decade to assume a position of greater prominence than ever before.

Later, we will examine the context in which this growth has taken place. But first a few words of introduction to the thing itself. We are talking about organizations for *ministry*; that is, those established precisely for the purpose of doing something specifically related to Christian mission. A secular multi-county development commission might engage in roughly the same activities as the Morgan-Scott Project for Cooperative Christian Concerns (see Chapter 7). But Morgan-Scott falls within the limits of our study and the commission does not, because Morgan-Scott is deliberately organized for work related to the Church's task.

3

The second indispensable mark of an area organization has been mentioned already. Not only must it minister, it must do so in a territory larger than a parish and smaller than a diocese or judicatory. ("Judicatory" is a generic term used to designate a level of Protestant church organization roughly equivalent to a Catholic diocese.) Such an organization might be large or small, simple or complex, formal or informal in organization. The only requirement is that it be a middle-level organization within the diocesan framework.

Area ministry is neither an exclusively rural nor an exclusively urban phenomenon. In its new forms, it has flourished in both settings since the late 1960's, first in the cities and then increasingly in nonmetropolitan places. Our interest is in the less densely-populated parts of America, however, and we will focus on rural area ministry, leaving urban organizations entirely to one side. The term "rural" has many definitions. For our purposes, it refers to area groups which operate wholly or largely in open countryside or in towns of 10,000 or less, away from cities, suburbs and urban fringes.

The danger in discussing any new thing, whether church-related or not, is that one is tempted to overemphasize its merits. It will solve all problems; it will permanently change the social institution of which it forms a part. With respect to area ministry, such claims would certainly betray a loss of perspective. Area organizations, after all, are only structures, important enough as vehicles for delivering needed services, but hardly capable of renewing the rural Church. More importantly, area organizations are by nature "between." They do not exist to supplant parish or diocese, but to strengthen and complement them. This is especially true with respect to the parish. As we shall see, one of the primary aims of the area ministry organization is to bolster the parish and make it more effective.

Area structures have developed in response to certain needs too specialized or complex for the parish to serve, yet too local to be met conveniently from the diocesan center. This is the most general conclusion to emerge from a recent survey of more than 100 area organizations in 28 states conducted by the Glenmary Research Center. Analysis shows that these needs fall naturally into three broad classes: the need for peer support for church workers in their lives and work, the need for better communication and consultation within the Church, and the need to strengthen and complement parish work. Accordingly, there are three types of area ministry organization: the support group, the advisory group and the action group.

Support Area Ministries. The support organization is quite simple in concept. It exists for the purpose of ministering to the ministers themselves, to church workers of all types, part-time or full-time, clerical, religious or lay. This ministry may vary from one group to the next. But essentially it responds to the desire for a community of peers that can enrich the life of rural church leaders and stimulate their work.

What services can such organizations offer? In answering this question, it is helpful to make a distinction between personal and professional support. The group can help satisfy its members' personal needs in many ways: by affirming their sense of worth, by reinforcing their world view, by providing an opportunity to form friendships, by offering recreational opportunities and, perhaps most importantly, by creating occasions for shared prayer and personal spiritual development. These functions do not necessarily involve much planning; a small number of people can perform them all simply by meeting on a regular basis.

Groups of this sort can also provide some forms of professional support. Their meetings can become arenas for the airing of mutual concerns. By sitting down and talking informally with people who have faced the same challenges they are facing, individual church workers develop creative new ideas for their own ministries. In the same way, they can pray together for the success of their work.

There is a whole range of professionally-oriented services, however, which require greater size and a somewhat higher level of organization. A support group, for example, can serve as a sophisticated medium for the exchange of professional information. And it can promote the continuing education of its members by sponsoring workshops and courses, by inviting speakers to its meetings and so on. This educational service is perhaps the most concrete professional aid a support group can provide, and it forms the core activity of many organizations.

Large area ministry groups have a marked tendency to gravitate toward direct apostolic work; only a few specialize in support. The Northeast Texas Clergy-Religious Group, described in Chapter 3, is one of the exceptions—a "pure" support organization whose members deliberately exclude all other functions. In the most common pattern, however, the larger organizations offer support as part of a more comprehensive program. The Town and Country Apostolic Council (Chapter 2) is primarily a support group which is also advisory, while the Deanery Three Council in the Diocese of Tulsa (Chapter 4) is the reverse—an advisory organization with support functions. The Leon Regional Catholic Community (Chapter 6), in large part a team ministry, combines an action orientation with significant support services. Finally, most of the regional conferences in the Diocese of Rochester (Chapter 9) are support organizations which are striving to develop both advisory and action functions.

Advisory Area Ministries. As we have seen, the support organization offers a ministry to church workers, professional or otherwise. It is an "in-house" sort of body. In a sense, so is the advisory organization, but its purpose is different. It exists to influence policy and encourage other units within the Church to undertake programs in the apostolate. A coalition of priests, for example, might be asked by a diocesan personnel board to comment on proposed guidelines for clergy assignments in rural areas. Or the same coalition might strongly urge the diocese to establish a special program for migrant farm workers.

The needs which advisory organizations fulfill is clear enough. Since Vatican II, growing emphasis has been laid on broad consultation within the Catholic Church as a means of insuring better decisions. Meanwhile, the spirit of the times continues to encourage a more wide-open approach to government in all the major Christian denominations. The advisory group contributes to this movement by serving as a link in a communications chain which feeds a wide spectrum of opinion into the decision-making process.

The value of the area advisory organization derives from its position as a middle-level body in a diocesan or judicatory structure. Because of distance and other factors, the diocese is often organizationally rather remote from the individual parish. If the advisory group functions properly, it can bridge this gap, giving local congregations a real voice in the diocese. By fostering greater participation, the advisory group not only works to improve the quality of decision-making, but it can also serve as a unifying device of real significance to the life of the ecclesial community.

As was mentioned earlier, the great majority of larger area ministries are "mixed" in character, performing more than one principal function. The survey referred to above did not uncover a single "pure" advisory group. Usually, when an area organization offers diversified services, one of them predominates over the others; the organization will be an advisory group with secondary support functions, for example, or a support group with minor action functions. This emphasis, which often develops spontaneously, allows the members to see their organization as having a unified purpose. Among the groups surveyed, Deanery Three Council (Chapter 4) is unique in that its primary reason for being is the giving of advice. The advisory function in other organizations varies from very important in the Town and Country Apostolic Council (Chapter 2) to significant in the regional conferences of the Diocese of Rochester (Chapter 9) to extremely minor in the Leon Regional Catholic Community (Chapter 6).

These same groups may be used to illustrate three sets of alternatives which are open to advisory organizations. Choices between these alternatives go far toward determining how a particular group will function within its judicatory or diocese. First, membership in the advisory body may be either mandatory or voluntary. In most cases, this distinction carries a secondary implication; mandatory organizations are usually established as official parts of a diocesan structure. Thus, the Rochester conferences are made up of representatives of all the parishes and other institutions in their areas and participation is mandatory. These conferences hold a recognized place in the diocese, forming the intermediary structure between the parish councils and the diocesan pastoral council. The Town and Country Apostolic Council, on the other hand, is a free association of volunteers that is in the Archdiocese of Louisville but not of it. The organization works closely with diocesan authorities but is neither ratified nor funded by them.

The second set of alternatives is not mutually exclusive like the first. The advisory group may make recommendations on its own and/or respond to a specific request. At various times, the Town and Country Apostolic Council has done both. So have Deanery Three Council and the Rochester conferences, some of which have constitutions which specify that they may speak out on an issue without awaiting an outside request.

Third, an advisory group can aim its advice across and down as well as up. We have spoken so far only of the relationship between area organization and diocese, since this is the primary consideration. But the advisory group can take advantage of its middle placement to make recommendations to parishes or even individuals on the parish level. It can also suggest that action be taken on its own level—that an area task force on evangelization be set up, for example. Deanery Three Council did just this; it has also made a whole range of recommendations to the parishes of the area.

Action Area Ministries. If the responsibility of the advisory organization is to urge other church groups to undertake programs in the apostolate, the task of the action organization is to operate such programs. Some action groups specialize in a particular sort of ministry; ecumenical ones, for example, more often than not focus exclusively on social ministry. This is purely a matter of individual choice, however. The theoretical range of an action organization covers the whole of the Church's mission.

We noted earlier that the general purpose of area action groups was to strengthen and complement parish programs. Rural parishes are beginning to realize that, even with the best of intentions, they cannot operate a completely effective ministry without outside help. Some of this help will come from the diocese—from the office of religious education, for example. But it is often more convenient to organize parish-oriented services at a lower level. Branch offices of diocesan agencies may be established to serve a certain number of parishes, or other area structures may be set up to supply the need. Thus, a small interparish group in Grants Pass, Oregon maintains a library of audio-visual equipment from which member parishes and others may borrow. The Rochester regional conferences (Chapter 9) are currently setting up a program which will enable parishes to upgrade their services to nursing homes.

And the Center for Community Organization and Area Development (Chapter 8) runs semi-annual institutes to help parishes toward greater involvement with their local communities.

The action organization also operates programs which are not specifically geared toward parishes, but which complement parish ministry in that they serve the same overall purpose. The Interchurch Coordinating Council in Missouri (Chapter 5) administers a RSVP program, for instance, which provides an opportunity for retired persons to volunteer for various kinds of public-spirited work. This project, besides being a source of creative ideas for parishes, generally improves the climate for launching parochial ministries to the elderly. There is a great need for programs to serve basic human needs in the mountains of eastern Tennessee, and parishes of various denominations run food pantries, clothing closets and the like as part of their ministry. At the same time, the Morgan-Scott Project (Chapter 7) sponsors a home missions committee which supplies similar services, thus filling out and extending the parishes' work.

Some of these complementary ministries are highly specialized. In addition to RSVP, the Interchurch Coordinating Council established a counseling service which provides professional help to the mentally disturbed. In addition to the home mission committee, the Morgan-Scott Project operates a state-approved school for children with learning disabilities. There is little likelihood that any parish would undertake tasks like these. Even if they could, it is debatable that they should; traditionally, the parish has focused on providing a broad ministry to all the people, not a series of intensive ministries to small, select groups. Nevertheless, such programs are clearly supplementary to parish social action and help define the area organization's place in the total mission of the rural Church.

Action organizations run the whole gamut of organizational complexity. Small action groups which operate only one or two modest programs can be structured very simply. But the action function has built-in characteristics which make it almost inevitable that the organization wishing to offer a wide range of services will have a highly developed structure. For one thing, action programs usually require substantial funding, in opposition to support and advisory programs. This means that the group must have some machinery for raising money. Action programs often require a good deal of administration, so the group must have administrative components. The successful operation of action programs may necessitate the hiring of a professional staff, which is in itself a structural elaboration. For these reasons and others, a large action organization can be a very complicated phenomenon. The Interchurch Coordinating Council (Chapter 5) has hundreds of members, a cabinet, an executive committee, a staff, an assembly, and a number of task forces which bear varied relationships to the other structural components.

According to the Glenmary Research Center survey, the most common action area ministry is the interparish organization. In this model, two or more parishes come together to accomplish what a single parish would find difficult or impossible. The most common form of interparish cooperation, in turn, is the joint operation of programs. Two neighboring rural parishes, for example, might each have only fifteen teenagers. A combined high school religion program would benefit both. Or again, there might be a great need in a given area for an organized ministry to the rural poor. The Catholic, Presbyterian, Lutheran and Methodist parishes could jointly hire professional staff to run a sophisticated program offering counseling and other help. (The ecumenical interparish organization is an exception to the rule that area ministry groups operate in a territory larger than a parish. It will often happen that such an organization will serve an area roughly coextensive with the mutual boundaries of its member congregations.)

Interparish programs are usually run by cooperative structures made up of delegates from the member congregations. But a group of parishes could also operate according to an arrangement called "part for the whole." Here, each party agrees to carry out one particular ministry, such as a social program for the elderly or a recreational program for youth. Although they are administered by individual parishes, each of these programs serves the entire area and is conducted in the name of all. This allows the parishes to pool their resources and avoid duplication of effort without creating additional administrative machinery.

For a variety of reasons, financial and otherwise, most interparish organizations do not provide a wide range of services. One rarely finds a group that operates as many as four major projects simultaneously, and cooperation can be restricted to something as simple as jointly sponsoring a series of Lenten talks. The average group sustains one or two projects requiring some permanent administration, such as a cooperative social ministry. Sometimes these organizations are established with a specific task in view and are limited in scope from the beginning. Others are established to take up whatever challenge comes along.

So far we have discussed interparish programs. There is another sort of interparish organization, that which provides a structure for the sharing of staff. Chapter 6 is devoted to a discussion of one such group, the Leon Regional Catholic Community. Leon's principal component is a team of three priests who serve as co-pastors of seven separate congregations. Although each parish is canonically separate from the others, the priests reside in a single rectory and share all work, just as though they were attached to the same parish. The Green River Interparish Ministry (Chapter 2), a six-person team serving four parishes in Kentucky, is set up in a different way. Two sisters who are religious education specialists and four priests share certain tasks involving all the member congregations. But the pastors exercise individual responsibility for their own parishes where, most of the time, they live and work alone. Leon provides an example of a closely integrated interparish staff and Green River of a loosely integrated one. In both models, the intent is to strengthen parish ministry by pooling human resources.

The action organizations which are not coalitions of parishes are difficult to classify neatly. To one side of the interparish grouping is the organization run by a single entity, whether it be a parish, an independent ministry or a diocese. One parish in western Kentucky has established a high school religious education program that children from other parishes attend. It is thus performing an area ministry. So is the Human/Economic Appalachian Development Corporation which, acting from motives of Christian concern, sponsors a program to train Appalachian people to run their own small businesses. Many dioceses have agencies which serve a certain area in a particular way: the Diocese of Ogdensburg operates regional religious education centers, for example, and the Diocese of Milwaukee staffs an area office for the Spanish apostolate.

On the other side of the interparish grouping lies a varied array of forms. Some organizations, like the Southeast Oklahoma Multi-County Project (Chapter 4), are associations of individuals who took it upon themselves to band together for a better rural ministry. Some, like the Valley Service Project of the Texas Council of Churches and the Interchurch Coordinating Council (Chapter 5), are associations of judicatories or their agencies. The regional conferences in the Diocese of Rochester (Chapter 9) are composed of representatives from parishes and other Catholic institutions. The Morgan-Scott Project (Chapter 7) is sponsored by a coalition of judicatories, parishes and individuals. In Taberg, New York, representatives of the local churches, community groups and the fire department make up a committee organized to aid poeple whose homes have been destroyed by fire. And the Center for Community Organization and Area Development (Chapter 8) is sponsored by individuals acting in concert with a liberal arts college in South Dakota. Any combination of individuals and/or institutions with the will and the resources can set up an action group, and so the range of future possibilities is very wide.

Support emphasis, advisory emphasis, action emphasis. As we have seen, the new forms of area ministry have developed as part of the Church's effort to offer more effective apostolic programs, obtain better decision-making and provide peer support for church leaders in their lives and work. Let us now focus our attention on the specifically rural environment. What role do such middle-level organizations play in achieving these goals in the changing context of nonmetropolitan America?

In the traditional rural social pattern, most of which was still intact as recently as 40 years ago, everyday life was lived among comparatively few people and within the confines of a relatively small area. The average person's basic needs—food, clothing, shelter, recreation—were satisfied by his family and community. In return, he contributed what he had to offer to the same family and community, cementing his place in a stable if limited society. For the citizen of yesterday's country town, life was organized on a relatively small scale.

Today the technological explosion has transformed the economic and social structure of the United States. While rural areas have been less severely affected than the cities, conditions in nonmetropolitan Iowa or Wyoming or Alabama are greatly different from what they were within the memories of many residents. The development of modern means of transportation, especially the automobile, has made it possible to trade an hour's time for 50 miles instead of the five miles one could travel via horse and buggy. Thus rural people are no longer confined to the boundaries of a single community for shopping, medical services, employment, social life. At the same time, being part of a modern industrial state has meant that the needs of the community are served by giant national and international corporations rather than sources in the community itself. The supermarket has replaced the country store. These changes, nostalgia aside, have been welcomed, and people have grown to expect the conveniences which large-scale organization makes possible.

The forces that have brought a new quality to life in rural America have also had an impact on the rural Church. While the spectacular growth of knowledge in recent years was building better mousetraps and creating better health care in the secular world, it was opening new vistas on Scripture, theology, liturgy, counseling and styles of ecclesiastical leadership. The existence of this body of advanced knowledge has raised people's expectations with respect to religious services, and church workers, too, have come to expect a more highly developed ministry of themselves. Since the automobile has made it possible for them to serve more people in a larger area, they have almost inevitably gravitated in the same direction as the society that surrounds them. They have begun to show an interest in bigness, to look to structures larger than the rural parish.

So far, however, the Church has avoided a major error to which American society in general seems prone: that of equating progress with size. There has been no rush to organize ministry at the highest possible level in order to attain what might prove to be an illusory efficiency. Any tendencies of this sort have been checked by the Church's continuing loyalty to the local congregation, which remains a small-scale organization in an increasingly large-scale world.

Within the parish, Christians satisfy one another's most elementary and common religious needs, and bear witness to the community at large. It is the place where the individual, located within a network of human relationships, is served as an integral person, rather than in some specialized way. Other church organizations may offer particular ministries such as retreats or marriage counseling, but the task of the parish is to maintain its rounded function as spiritual guide and spiritual home, providing a stable center for the Christian's everyday life.

The pressure generated by people's rising expectations with respect to ministry and the resultant move toward larger, more efficient structures is very real. However, it would be a mistake to allow this pressure to affect the parish directly. If the local congregation were required to take on tasks which called for the employment of wide and varied resources or for extensive specialization, it would be in danger of losing its distinctive quality as a vehicle for basic ministry.

The Church must look outside the parochial framework, then, for a response to the modern challenge of increasing scale. Structures to meet this challenge will be found at all levels—area, diocesan, national and international. But there is a distinct advantage to structuring ministries that strengthen or complement parish programs as far down the organizational scale as their complexity will permit. At the area level they are as close as possible to the parish and potentially most responsive to its influence. Here the action area organization finds its place.

The role of the advisory area organization in the rural Church rests on a different set of premises. Collegial consultation in decision-making can have maximum impact only where the consulting elements are not too far removed from one another. If an individual writes a letter to the president of the United States, it may have little effect. On the other hand, if the individual joins with other like-minded citizens to advocate some position, and this group joins with others to form a national coalition, and this coalition writes a letter to the president, the matter is likely to receive careful consideration. The area organization can distill the opinions of pastors and parishioners and funnel them upward, bringing parish and diocese closer together. It therefore makes possible a greater exercise of practical collegiality within the diocesan structure.

If the automobile has enabled rural church workers to come together for service and for consultation, it has also allowed them to gather for mutual support. In the small town of the past, the priests or sisters had to satisfy their social needs exclusively within the community. These local ties continue to be valuable, of course. But today church people can form area support groups which expand their opportunities for personal and professional relationships with peers. Such organizations provide settings close to the parish for greater educational, spiritual and human development than were available a few generations ago.

Although area ministry could not have arisen without an increase in the scale of rural social organization, it has significance apart from this context. Within the past few years, the idea of community has become much more prominent in church circles; people want to work closely with others rather than operate entirely on their own. Area organizations of all kinds help meet this desire. They also expand the total range of the Church's ministry by allowing people and institutions to accomplish together what it would be difficult or impossible to accomplish alone. They demonstrate the feasibility of cooperation both within denominations and across denominational lines. Finally, from a purely practical point of view, they help compensate for the growing shortage of clergy by lending support to parishes.

It would be claiming too much to say that the rural Church in America is undergoing a renewal. But there are signs that the small town and open countryside are receiving more ministerial attention, at least from the traditionally urban-oriented Catholic Church. Diocesan agencies in many places are making their presence felt more decisively outside the cities. Sisters in increasing numbers are contracting to work in rural parishes as members of pastoral teams. Some parishes are being subdivided or combined. Finally, greater stress is being laid on the development of lay leadership, which holds out promise for the future.

Area ministry is a part of this stir of activity. The organizations whose histories are chronicled in the following pages started as experiments, as pioneering attempts to approach the old challenge of effective Christian witness in a new way. Although all of them have had some success, they are not models for imitation. If they were, they could only serve to stifle creativity, and in the rapidly expanding field of area ministry creativity is essential. The organizations are rather modest signposts that point in new directions.

2. The Search for Identity

*The Town and Country Apostolic Council
in the Archdiocese of Louisville*

It is not hard to understand why settlers in the late eighteenth century unhitched their wagons and made homes for themselves in central Kentucky. Coming down from the rocky ridges of the Appalachians, they must have seen this green rolling land with its cheerful streams much as Moses' people saw the land of Canaan. It was the promise fulfilled, the incarnation of the original American Dream. Here was "elbow room" unlimited, here was freedom from the relatively cramped world of the seaboard, here was the opportunity to "make something of ourselves." A man and his family could camp by a still grove, could build their cabin and, by accepting the challenge of the wilderness, could tame it and make it their own.

This lovely country, scene of operations for the Town and Country Apostolic Council (TACA), has a rather unusual religious geography. Catholics from Pennsylvania settled the section out of which Nelson, Washington and Marion counties were later carved. A parish, Holy Cross, was already flourishing by 1785, and the first Catholic diocese west of the Alleghenies was established at Bardstown in 1808. Civilization came to the rest of the region with Protestants from the eastern seaboard who established their own settlements, very separate from those of the Catholics. From the religious point of view, TACA's home area is really two areas, the first about 40 percent Catholic and the other, much larger, about 98 percent non-Catholic.

There are other contrasts within the region, but they are less important than the similarities. The counties to the south and east tend to be "Appalachian" in character; they are rugged and iso-

17

lated, their population is low, poverty and unemployment are high. The more northern counties are prosperous by comparison. An older, more settled culture dominates this section and a steady stream of tourists strengthens its economy. The prosperity of the north is only relative, however. The area as a whole is typical of rural America—a little tired, a little down at the heels, not poor exactly but certainly not very rich. Certain small cities like Bardstown, Somerset and Campbellsville are growing fast, but at the same time a lot of smaller towns are visibly dying. Rural central Kentucky is clearly benefiting from industry's recent trend toward expansion into the country; poverty levels have dropped dramatically in the past few years. But basically it is still a backwater, less well off, less privileged, less attended to, less worked with, than the great urban centers.

TACA was founded out of concern for the problems, religious and social, of this large and varied area, which forms part of the Archdiocese of Louisville. "Founded," though, is not really the right word. TACA evolved; it was an experiment that grew out of a previous experiment. Before we can discuss the Town and Country Apostolic Council, we must glance at another area organization, the Lebanon Area Conference of Priests (LACP).

The Conference arose from the initiative of one man. In May of 1969, the priests of the Lebanon deanery met to discuss a proposed pastoral council. Among them was Father C. Patrick Creed, who had recently been transferred from an urban parish in Louisville to a very rural one in Casey County. He had become increasingly frustrated by the conditions he found prevailing in the rural ministry. It seemed to him that inferior facilities, complacent congregations and the simple loneliness of isolated rectories had affected the morale of the clergy. Moreover, each rural priest was clearly on his own. There was no provision for personal or professional support, no shadow of a cooperative plan for rural ministry. A few exceptional men could function well under these conditions. One priest in particular spent the hours he could spare from parish work supervising the design and construction of recreational areas for young people. But compared to the city, action was relatively slow in the ministry.

Father Creed felt that the first prerequisite for breaking the spell was communication. If the priests were in closer contact with one another and had some means of sharing professional concerns, they would probably be happier. More importantly, they would develop creative ideas for ministry together. Each man could thus contribute to the work of his fellow priests and at the same time receive help, support and encouragement from them. As the deanery meeting ended, Father proposed that the priests meet again in two weeks to form an organization of their own. To his considerable surprise, the suggestion was immediately accepted. He had hit a nerve.

The first meeting of LACP was held May 21, 1969, with 19 priests in attendance. As it finally worked out, the new organization covered all of one deanery and a bit of another—14 counties, altogether. It lived for about a year and a half, and during this time its membership averaged 20. Father Creed was the group's first and only president; he remained the central figure in its operation as long as it lasted.

LACP's charter members adopted the two goals Father Creed had in mind for the organization and added one more. The Conference would bring priests together for fellowship and support and would provide a place where matters of mutual concern could be aired. It would also go a step further and sponsor a series of educational programs to keep the priests informed on matters related to the ministry. The meetings were largely social in character. The members gathered, joined in a worship service of some kind, talked among themselves, exchanged ideas, perhaps listened to an invited speaker. In June of 1969 the priests engaged in a discussion of the new funeral rite, while the meeting for April 1970 was devoted to a program presented by the Social Action Committee of the archdiocese.

Although it did administer one small apostolic program, the Lebanon Area Conference was essentially a support group. From all indications, it succeeded admirably in its role. The members who were present from the beginning recall the meetings fondly as warm, informal get-togethers at which a great deal of useful information was exchanged and pressure was at a minimum. Archbishop Thomas McDonough and his staff were happy with the Conference because it facilitated communication with the rural priests. An expert in religious education, say, could be sent to address one or two meetings of the group instead of painstakingly making the rounds of all the parishes. In the same way, if a workshop or seminar for the whole diocese were being held in Louisville, the Conference could assign representatives to attend it and report back to the full membership at the next meeting. Thus a great deal of travel time was saved all around. It was a good system and it functioned well through 1969 and much of 1970.

But there were forces at work within the organization that in a relatively short time would force its evolution into the Town and Country Apostolic Council. By far the most significant of these forces was the will to action. A number of the members, Father Creed among them, were growing discontented with LACP's "members only" support orientation. They wanted to direct the organization outward, to work on other people's problems as well as their own, to develop and operate apostolic programs.

Opposition to this way of thinking was strong among the priests who wanted LACP to remain as it was, and they might well have prevailed had not certain events occurred to hasten change. On November 10-12, 1970, LACP sponsored a workshop on "Open Space Ministry" at Nazareth, Kentucky that was attended by about 65 rural church workers. The speakers dealt with rural ministry in general, but a substantial portion of their presentation focussed directly on area organizations. They pointed out that such groups could form a new organizational level within dioceses, pursuing support and action goals that were too narrow in scope to arouse the concern of diocesan authorities but at the same time too broad to be pursued by individual parishes.

Through this workshop, the Conference first confronted the concrete possibility of becoming an action organization. That possibility became a reality by means of a second happening, one which hardly seemed calculated to have dramatic results. Several months before the workshop was given, a team ministry involving three priests and four sisters had been set up at Somerset. The Conference's meetings were held at various rectories on a rotating basis. When it next met in Somerset, the team sisters were invited to attend. This simple act of courtesy signalled the end of LACP.

The sisters who sat in on the meeting that day had no designs on

LACP, but their presence had the effect of throwing the question of eligibility for membership wide open. Although LACP had been composed of priests only, no guidelines had ever been adopted specifically restricting membership to the clergy. It soon became clear, moreover, that the sisters considered themselves rural ministers no less than the priests, and therefore qualified to participate in an organization of rural ministers. The issue of admitting sisters was discussed, the move was approved by a majority vote and, within a short time, sisters outnumbered priests at Conference meetings.

This rapid expansion of membership had several important consequences for LACP. The name of the organization became immediately obsolete, for one thing; no longer was it a Conference of Priests. And, in the minds of some, that fact alone was of the greatest significance. It meant that the Conference had ceased to be an association of men with similar interests and concerns. It meant that the fellowship and mutual support that the group had provided were badly weakened if not destroyed. Perhaps half of all the pastors belonging to LACP withdrew, greatly reducing its representation in the parishes.

At the same time, most of the sisters were action-oriented. They recognized the value of LACP's social and educational objectives, but did not feel that these objectives should be given first priority. Their inclusion in the group decisively strengthened the position of those priests who had been trying to steer the Conference in a new direction and provided the final push that transformed it into the Town and Country Apostolic Council.

The change over from LACP to TACA does not seem to have been especially smooth. There was a good deal of uncertainty toward the end of 1970 as the members, realizing that the Conference was dead, sought for a new concept around which to build a new organization. Some people thought the support activities the Conference had sponsored were perfectly valid and should be continued, while others were all for forgetting support and concentrating on action alone. With so diverse a group, some compromise was necessary, but finding a workable one was not easy.

Finally, a formula was hammered out. The new body would be open not only to clergy, but to religious and laity as well. The support function would be retained, but it would be de-emphasized and the Council would consider itself an organization primarily dedicated to active ministry. Particular stress would be placed on the concept of cooperative ministry set forth at the Nazareth workshop. On January 4, 1971, a meeting of interested priests and sisters adopted a set of interim guidelines for a new structure, and the Town and Country Apostolic Council was officially formed.

Unlike the Conference, TACA initially was envisioned as covering the entire rural part of the archdiocese with the exception of those extreme northern counties which lay close to Louisville. This area included 24 counties and numbered 29 parishes within its borders. Because the members felt that their organization, in spite of its size, should remain in close touch with people, they subdivided it into five district planning groups. These district units, which met independently at a time set aside for this purpose within the Council's regular meetings, were organized with about seven members each.

Structurally, then, TACA consisted of a general membership divided into district units which approximated standing committees. Each individual was both a member of the general assembly (the Council as a whole) and one of the district units. The membership elected a president and treasurer and empowered the president to appoint a board of directors. Two stipulations were made: first, that the board be representative of the whole area; and second, that at least one sister be appointed. Not surprisingly, Father Creed was elected president and he named the board in March 1971.

The relationship between board and general assembly was not spelled out in the guidelines, but a practical division of power soon emerged. TACA's assembly alone can make policy and the assembly holds the ultimate executive power in matters of importance. Even if a certain move is approved by the board, it still has to be approved by the assembly before it can be implemented. Both the whole assembly or its committees—the district units and the various committees that succeeded them after 1971—can originate, develop and implement projects, on the other hand, without the formal approval of the board.

The power of the board, which is considerable, has a double

base. First, it handles all routine TACA business that does not require a policy decision, such as communicating with the archdiocese or some other outside organization. Second, it can focus TACA on certain problems and guide it in certain directions. Although assembly committees can, and sometimes do, carry through projects without referring them to the board, in practice most major proposals pass before that body. By approving or disapproving a given proposal, the board can influence the assembly's vote on it. Also, by originating questions for the assembly to deal with, the board sees to it that the issues it considers significant receive attention. Despite having only minor executive power, the board of directors does provide leadership.

No agendas or minutes for the district group meetings survive, but some idea of TACA's activities during 1971 may be gleaned from agendas of the larger Council meetings. On each occasion, the first item of business was a worship service, usually Benediction. This was followed by some educational program. In March the program consisted of a series of talks by different members on changes in the liturgy for Holy Week and on the use of the Roman Missal. In May it was a presentation by the archdiocesan director of religious education on plans his office was making for 1971 and 1972. Following a coffee break, members split up for the district meetings and, when the group reconvened as a whole, reports on these meetings were given. The last hour or so was devoted to business that concerned the entire Council, such as election of officers or discussion of a policy step. The meetings were held in the afternoon, usually on weekdays, and lasted three to four hours. TACA met monthly except during July and August, when the members enjoyed a summer recess.

Clearly, these activities are not very different from those which TACA's predecessor, the Lebanon Area Conference, had pursued in previous years. In spite of the action orientation of the new guidelines, TACA did not move from the ground the Conference had occupied until it had been in existence for some time. However the rhetoric had changed, the emphasis remained in practice on mutual support and the continuing education of the members. TACA did not even maintain the one apostolic program that LACP had administered.

There are many reasons for TACA's inertia in its first year. One is the tendency of any organization that occupies a particular position to remain in that position. It is familiar, it is safe, its very continuity breeds a sense of security. A second is the fact that not all the individuals who favored the Conference's mode of operation had left when that organization dissolved, and these members exerted an influence that discouraged change. Third, the heated conflict of the previous fall between advocates of action and advocates of support was still in everyone's mind, and the group was not willing to risk renewing that conflict so soon.

There was also another conflict, more personal, potentially more dangerous, that affected TACA's performance at this stage. As we have seen, many priests resented the fact that sisters had joined what had been an all-clergy organization, changing it radically. The two groups, or at least substantial blocs in each group, tended to remain at odds through much of 1971.

Much of the ill feeling between them grew out of their relationships in the pre-Vatican II Church. In the past priests and sisters have normally had their separate jobs. Priests did such things as run the parishes, teach at boys' schools at the secondary level or above, and perform special tasks for their orders; while sisters staffed hospitals, did charity work, taught in girl's schools. When the two did render service together—as, for example, in parish work or teaching—priests generally held the decision-making power and the sisters were looked upon as helpers.

The sisters who came into the Conference and contributed to the creation of TACA, though not markedly aggressive as a group, had quite a different vision of their ministerial roles. They were not interested in assuming a subordinate position within TACA. As a result, all the members of the new organization were faced with the necessity not only of coexisting but of cooperating, and of cooperating as equals. For many, men and women, this was a new experience and it is not surprising that tensions arose. TACA's later history shows that the situation worked itself out, but for a time it was a singularly touchy one and absorbed much of the members' attention.

The last two causes of TACA's slow start are connected with the nuts and bolts of the organization. First, in the interim guidelines accepted at the beginning of the year, TACA's purpose was stated to be "to coordinate apostolic efforts among the various ministers serving the town and country apostolate . . . of the Archdiocese of Louisville, in order to establish mutual sharing and execution of apostolic goals." If a realistic purpose may be defined as one commensurate with an organization's power to perform, this purpose was manifestly unrealistic. TACA could not coordinate apostolic efforts among those serving the rural part of the archdiocese unless it represented them all or had some sort of authority over them. In fact, a large percentage of the pastors, to say nothing of the sisters and lay leaders, were not members of TACA, did not consider themselves to be represented by TACA, admitted no allegiance to TACA of any kind. Clearly, the Council represented only its own members, a relatively small group of volunteers.

This contradiction did not go unnoticed by the membership. But instead of restating TACA's purpose, they decided that the Council should "seek to be representative of the entire rural area [of the archdiocese]." In practice this was impossible; the strife caused by the dissolution of the Conference alone would have prevented TACA from becoming truly representative. It was also a distraction. As long as the members were wasting energy trying to be representative of the whole area, they could not concentrate on pursuing a more realistic goal. They had put themselves in a position which, by its very nature, caused frustration, confusion and at least mild organizational paralysis.

The second organizational problem took longer to surface. By the fall of 1971, however, it was becoming clear that the decision to subdivide the Council into district units had backfired. So few people were available for district meetings on any given day, and each district presented such a confusing array of problems, that the units could do nothing. No priorities had been set to help group members decide which problems to tackle first. Besides, there was general uncertainty about what could be done even if groups did decide to work in a particular area. As far as action programs were concerned, TACA was not set up to function effectively.

Although the resolution of all the rest of TACA's problems could be delayed without putting it in any acute danger, this misalignment had to be corrected immediately. The structure adopted in

January had been established on a temporary basis only, and as winter approached TACA began the process of working out a more permanent arrangement for the future. On November 8, the district groups met and drew up a series of proposals for the consideration of the board of directors. At its meeting some two weeks later, the board examined these proposals and decided that it would be best to drop the district groups altogether and to reorganize TACA along the lines of a parish council. Father Joseph Voor, head of the Commission on Councils for the archdiocese, had recently issued a booklet on "Your Parish Council" and the board felt that the structure it described would work for TACA. On December 13, 1971, this reorganization plan was submitted to the full Council and accepted.

So ended TACA's first structural phase and its first year of life. From the viewpoint of those interested in aggressive action programs, it must have seemed that little had been accomplished. But to expect real apostolic action from an organization with several serious problems was unrealistic and unfair. The other aims of the Council—to provide fellowship, support and opportunities for continuing education to its own members—were being fulfilled admirably. Most importantly, the members began to develop a sense of solidarity and a deeper commitment to the ministerial needs of the rural Church in the archdiocese.

The reorganization of the Council was accomplished with little fanfare and a great deal of efficiency. The board of directors and the offices of president, treasurer and secretary were retained as structural elements. But the members, with the exception of a few individuals who chose to be "at large," formed themselves into four standing committees—Formation, Administration, Worship and Service—as Father Voor's booklet suggested. Each committee had a fairly specific area of responsibility in the setting and execution of Council policy. Formation was to focus primarily on the education of TACA people, though its members had hopes of conducting programs for the area parishes as well. Service was to deal in action projects for the area community as a whole and for the parishes. Administration took on the task not only of supervising the Council's internal operations and financial affairs but also of giving the parishes financial advice. Finally, Worship would plan and lead the services which were a part of each Council meeting and would offer the parishes help in updating their liturgical practices.

As these job descriptions for the committees show, TACA's general orientation did not change as it moved from its first phase to its second. TACA in 1971 was supposed to be an area organization involved in both support and action, and it continued to be envisioned this way in 1972. The Formation and Worship Committees were charged with carrying on the support function, while Service was given the primary responsibility for developing action programs. But, while TACA in 1971 had been unable to perform this double duty, the restructured Council was quite successful. Inevitably, some confusion resulted from the major transformation the Council underwent; all the new committees except Worship were still trying to clarify their objectives in April of 1972. Despite this lack of precise focus, however, TACA made significant progress in the first six months of the year. The great conflicts that had plagued the organization earlier were gradually absorbed and neutralized in the pursuit of its ministry. Blessed with relative peace and a more workable structure, TACA moved toward unifying the nonmetropolitan Church workers.

The most striking indication of TACA's new health in 1972 was its physical growth. In January there were 38 members, the same number as had been active in mid-1971. But by June Father Creed could report to the archbishop that over the first half of 1972 an average of 65 had attended meetings, and in November the membership list contained 78 names.

There was a similar upsurge in activities of various kinds. In an attempt to clarify (and perhaps limit) TACA's purpose, the board in March attached a list of more or less specific objectives to the guidelines of the organization. These helped stimulate new creative efforts in several different directions. Some projects did not work out as their sponsors hoped. It occurred to the Administration Committee, for example, that individual parishes might set up credit unions for the use of the community. They researched this possibility through February and worked out a plan for providing seed-money from the Archdiocesan Development Emergency Fund. The committee also offered to put interested parishes in contact with an outside expert who would help get credit unions started. But no applications came in and the project was dropped in April.

Most of TACA's projects produced more positive results. The services that the organization provided for its own members—support, fellowship, education—increased in value as TACA grew in size and became more tightly knit. It is one thing to draw support from a gathering of 35 people who are not sure what their purpose is, as in 1971, and quite another to feel oneself part of a group of 60 or 70 with a strong sense of mission. The difference is nowhere more clearly evident than in the worship services in which the members were participating at this time. In the past, Benediction had been the most common form of worship TACA used. This is a familiar ritual and a Catholic can participate almost from habit. But beginning in April 1972, under the aegis of the Worship Committee, TACA meetings were highlighted by semiformal, "personalized" prayer services, prepared by Council members and directed toward Council concerns. The emphasis which the members of TACA placed on worship, certainly appropriate to a Christian ministry group, perhaps did more to stabilize the organization than any other features of its corporate life.

Among the organization's educational projects, one stands out as especially worthy of note. It may have been prompted by the tension between sisters and priests which TACA had experienced, even though it was not aimed exclusively at Council members. In January, planning began for a Pastoral/Team Ministry Institute that was concerned, among other things, with the ways sisters could work with the clergy in parishes. This two-month course, that was sponsored jointly by TACA and Bellarmine College in Louisville, was held during the summer and was well attended.

Some success was also achieved in action programs. For one thing, permission to resume the local administration of Archdiocesan Development Fund money, a project that had originated with the Lebanon Area Conference but had been dropped in 1971, was obtained. This involved disbursing some $16,000 in poverty aid to area parishes, both on a routine basis and in response to emergencies. At about the same time, a delegation from TACA went to Archbishop McDonough and obtained a substantial grant for St.

Mary's Seminary which, like so many private colleges across the country, was having trouble making ends meet.

TACA became actively interested in the proceedings of the Kentucky legislature in early 1972. In January and February, the members discussed impending legislation on abortion and poverty, and a bill providing tax breaks for parents with children in parochial schools received attention in March. Through a member of the Service Committee, TACA obtained access to a lobbyist's reports on the progress of anti-poverty legislation at the capitol. The news was not encouraging and the membership directed Father Creed to write to Governor Ford, urging executive action on two stalled bills.

At this time, TACA quite unconsciously began to behave like an advisory organization as well, even though it was technically oriented only toward support and action. Religious education had been a concern of all the parishes in the area for years. Many parochial schools had closed and there was a general lack of trained teachers for religious instruction at all levels, child and adult. This problem had often been the subject of discussion at TACA meetings, but the organization simply did not have the resources or the authority to deal with it independently. In 1971, however, Father J. Kendrick Williams, a member of TACA's board, developed an experimental religious education program designed for four selected parishes. Through the efforts of the Council, he, Sister Elizabeth Wendeln, S.C.N. (also a board member) and Sister Elizabeth Glynn, O.P. were appointed to the Archdiocesan Office of Religious Education.

Lengthy negotiations followed, ending in approval for the founding of a branch office of this agency which would focus on the education problems of the nonmetropolitan area. On June 1, 1972, the Rural Office of Religious Education was opened at Nazareth with Father Williams as director. The establishment of this office was quite a significant accomplishment for TACA. The organization had shown itself to be an effective force in the archdiocese for strengthening parish ministry.

The Council's meeting in June of 1972 was a happy occasion. There was a definite sense of progress in the air and the future seemed bright. But when the members returned from their customary summer recess, they found that TACA's situation had drastically changed. On August 24, Father Creed received a letter from Father Voor of the Commission on Councils outlining plans for the formation of ten official, mandated area councils throughout the archdiocese as a first step toward evolving a pastoral council. Action aimed at organizing these bodies would begin in September and Father Voor wanted TACA to play a leading role in setting them up in rural areas. Few TACA people were against the proposed groups; indeed, their establishment had been foreseen. But the announcement that the archdiocese was suddenly ready to move on the project took TACA by surprise and an atmosphere of crisis rapidly developed in the wake of Father Voor's letter.

On the very day he received the unexpected news, Father Creed wrote in turn to all the rural priests, whether they were members of TACA or not, explaining the situation and calling a meeting to determine what course of action the Council should take. In order to test the strength of the commitment these men had to TACA, Father said in his letter that the goals of the proposed area councils were virtually identical with TACA's and that therefore TACA should consider disbanding. Much to his satisfaction, the priests, when they met on August 29, rejected this suggestion out of hand. In a dramatic display of support for the organization, they recommended unanimously that TACA remain in business and attempt to work out some sort of compromise arrangement with the new area structure. This decision was upheld when the Council next met on October 8.

TACA went into a state of shock at this sudden turn of events, but the next few months were not a complete loss. A speaker was invited to present a program on ecumenism at the November meeting. During November, also, TACA worked with the archdiocese's Liturgical Commission to set up a meeting at which the provisional sacramentary was explained to area priests, and in December a list of proposed recommendations to the Senate of Priests and the Senate of Religious was discussed. The most potentially significant accomplishment of this period looked to the future. Council members adopted *Quest for Justice*, the report of the world synod of 1971, as a starting point for problem discovery and service in 1973.

By the time the new year arrived, however, TACA was too paralysed to follow up on this new thrust. The Worship Committee did move to create a workshop for lectors which could be given in any parish that requested it. In addition, arrangements were made for a second Pastoral/Team Ministry Institute to be held during the summer. But no other plans were implemented, and TACA actually lost one active program. Disagreements developed over the handling of the Archdiocesan Development Fund money and in February the membership voted to return administration of this fund to the deaneries.

Soon, the Council was foundering in a sea of confusion. Its January meeting had been cancelled because of a possible conflict with the proposed meeting dates of the area councils; now the April and May meetings were called off for the same reason. The board, ignoring the previous decision to make *Quest for Justice* the basis for future endeavors, agreed in February that TACA's main thrust in 1973 should be helping the area councils emerge. But these new bodies still existed only on paper and no one knew how to proceed. Meanwhile, TACA was trying vainly to run its own programs, independently of the mandated councils. It is not surprising that the membership voted in March to abandon the interim guidelines and draw up a constitution. By this time the organization had clearly departed from its original purpose and new guidelines were needed to express its future goal.

That new goal was difficult to define, however, because somewhere along the line TACA had lost its identity. Was it a semi-autonomous agency with programs of its own, as its actual operations implied? Or was it a completely subordinate group whose principal function was to serve the area councils, as the board's most recent statement held? At the May board meeting, the question was put with simplicity and force: "It was suggested that TACA zero in on one point and choose one goal. Being all things to all men is impossible. It was considered necessary to decide if TACA should be alive or dead. It seemed desirable to continue [but to continue] anew." The board and the chairmen of the standing committees drew up a list of eight alternatives for the future which ranged from a proposal to dissolve TACA altogether to a proposal for preserving the status quo.

Three of the alternatives, which avoided both these extremes, opened up the possibility of a whole new thrust for the Council. The first was to the effect that TACA could survive as a social group having influence in archdiocesan affairs. The second suggested that TACA could meet to celebrate the liturgy with skill, creativity and devotion. The third proposed that the Council become a support organization whose principal function would be to maintain that spirit of cooperation among rural Church workers which had grown up since 1969. On June 10, 1973, the members voted to abandon the parish council model they had followed for eighteen months and to make TACA over with a philosophy and structure that incorporated elements of all these ideas.

Thus the second phase of TACA's life came to a close. The end of this period coincided with the end of Father Creed's active involvement with the organization. Early in June he received word that he was being transferred to a parish in Louisville. Father Creed's service to the Council, and to the Conference of Priests before it, had been long and faithful. He had been the principal creative force behind both organizations and had guided them through some very difficult times. Just as the June 10 meeting adjourned, Father Creed expressed his appreciation to the members for the support they had given him over the years. They responded with a standing ovation.

In its third phase, TACA became what it is today, a support and advisory group. The resolution that effected the changeover to the new form read in part as follows: "That TACA emphasize the growth of its members along spiritual, social and intellectual lines and focus on one topic of concern at each meeting which will involve the entire group. Action will be in the form of recommendations sent to those in authority." The wording of this brief statement was precise and it had strong results. Since 1971, the Council's primary focus, in theory at least, had been on those outside the organization. Now it shifted to the members themselves. Since the meetings had to center around a single topic involving the whole group, the four standing committees into which the members had divided themselves were automatically dissolved. And, since action had to be confined to drawing up recommendations, all TACA's projects were automatically terminated. It was quite a complete transformation.

TACA's third phase may appear at first glance to be a step backwards. By giving up all direct action programs, the organization seemed to be returning to its early days in 1971 when, in practice if not in theory, it had concentrated solely on support. Had TACA really gone full circle, proving so weak that it could do no better than end where it began?

Not at all. For one thing, TACA did not become a support group again. It became a support and advisory group. So there was a fundamental difference in purpose and function between TACA, first phase, and TACA, third phase. There was also a great difference in the quality of function, as we shall see. By mid-1973 TACA was not the confused, divided band that had come together on January 4, 1971. It was a mature and highly conscious area ministry group that knew where it was going and had some definite ideas on how to get there.

When the reorganized Council convened after the summer recess in September 1973, certain matters demanded immediate attention. For one thing, TACA's structure and general purpose having been simplified, its meetings had to be redesigned. The organization had always relied on curious Chinese-box meetings to carry on its ordinary business, committee meetings being held within the larger Council meetings. When the standing committees were abolished, this format automatically became obsolete and was dropped. After a few months, TACA revived the practice of setting up committees, but did not go back to the old system of meetings within meetings. Instead, committee meetings were held separately from meetings of the Council. They were usually scheduled a week or two in advance so that reports of committee activities could be prepared and given to the full Council when it met. The length of the monthly meetings of the entire Council was set at three hours, about evenly divided among worship, educational activity, a meal and business.

TACA spent most of that autumn getting squared away and laying plans for the future. The meetings of September through November were occupied with the organizational matters just described and others—appointments to committees, suggested procedures, suggested goals. Father Williams, who had been chosen interim president when Father Creed went to Louisville, was elected to a full term of his own and a new board of directors was voted in.

It was not until December that the organization could really start performing its ministry and it did so by initiating educational programs. By policy, Council meeting time was to be devoted to listening to a principal speaker give a presentation on some matter of general interest, and "ministry sharing," where one member of TACA would explain the joys and difficulties of his particular work. In December, a state legislator called the Council's attention to a number of the issues (abortion, capital punishment, aid to private schools) before the Kentucky General Assembly. His talk was followed by "sharing" by Father Ron Knott, a former board member, who detailed some of his experiences as campus minister at a community college.

Thus TACA's year ended. The history of that year would not be complete, however, without some mention of the fact that in 1973 the Council became a godparent. In order to understand how this could be, we must go back some distance in time. In December of 1972, the pastors of four area parishes centering around Campbellsville announced that they had formed a team and would cooperatively plan Mass, confessional and preaching schedules. They also agreed to exchange valuable information and to make themselves available to serve one another's parishioners should the need arise. This team, which was actually a separate area ministry organization, became operative early in 1973 and proved to be quite a success.

After it had been in existence for some months, the pastors decided to broaden their base of operations by jointly hiring two sisters to run the religious education programs in their parishes. With the addition of this new dimension of service, the members felt that their group deserved a new name and so, in September 1973, the Campbellsville team became the Green River Inter-Parish Ministry (GRIP). Most of the members of this infant organization were also TACA members. Moreover, TACA could claim that it had prepared the ground for GRIP by sponsoring the

Pastoral/Team Ministry Institutes and by stimulating a willingness to cooperate among rural clergy and religious. GRIP was TACA's child almost as much as it was the child of its six creators.

By the time 1973 became 1974, TACA had successfully completed its changeover from all-purpose ministry organization to support and advisory organization. As mentioned, the support functions of the group had been initiated in December. At about the same time, standing and *ad hoc* committees were being established to help care for TACA's internal operations and carry out its advisory role. In January, the following committees began operations: Communications, which was responsible for membership and public relations; Constitution and Bylaws, which was charged with updating TACA's guidelines; Program, which decided on the time, place and educational topics for each meeting; Ecumenical, which was to explore possibilities for interdenominational contact in the area; Research on Family Relations, which was supposed to find out what need there was for family counseling in the area; Theology of Mission Workshop, which was appointed to make arrangements for a workshop; and Personnel Policies, which had the task of making recommendations to the Archdiocesan Personnel Commission on assignment of clergy to nonmetropolitan parishes. In order to increase further its impact on archdiocesan policy-making, TACA had also established official liaison with the New Forms of Ministry Committee, the Senate of Religious, the Priests' Senate, the Campaign for Human Development, the Archdiocesan Commission on Councils and the Archdiocesan Commission on Peace and Justice.

Thanks to the efforts of its committees on internal affairs and the overall guidance of the board of directors, TACA has been able to avoid any major operational problems since it entered its third phase. The work of two of these three committees was completed within a year or so. The Communications Committee spent most of its time preparing and distributing an informational brochure on TACA. Also, in April of 1974, it revised and updated TACA's mailing list, leading to a decision by the board to send copies of the minutes of the Council's meetings to such officials as the archbishop, the directors of various agencies and commissions, deans, senators and any liaison people designated by religious communities. Finally, Communications compiled a telephone directory for the convenience of all members. The Constitution and Bylaws Committee performed its assigned task quickly and efficiently. Planning for the revised guidelines got underway in January. A draft was submitted to the membership in April and, with minor changes, was promptly adopted. (For text see Appendix B.)

The Program Committee, which is made up of the board plus six people drawn from the general membership, continues to plan TACA's meetings, keeping the organization's educational campaign spinning along smoothly. A wide variety of topics and speakers has been featured during the past two and a half years. In the spring of 1974, Archbishop McDonough gave the Council some perspective on the long-range planning he and his staff were engaged in. Later that year the group heard two prominent sisters discuss the role of women in today's Church. The highlights of 1975 were presentations by a leading member of the National Farmers' Organization on "Reconciliation, Justice and Farm Issues," by a staffer from the Kentucky Commission on Human Rights on "Reconciliation and Race Relations" and by a panel of TACA members on a conference on evangelization which they had recently attended. The educational thrust for 1976 is ministry, and so far TACA has studied such subjects as a theology of Church, the development of the ministry of the laity and creative innovations in ministry.

As we have noted, the Council intended not only to make use of speakers but also to stimulate the members' imaginations through "ministry sharing" at each meeting. This practice was abandoned toward the end of 1974, but while it lasted such topics as the following were covered: the apostolate to the deaf; the history of Holy Cross parish, which is the oldest in Kentucky; the growth of GRIP; the techniques being used to prepare seminarians for the modern apostolate; and the educational programs of the Sisters of Charity at Nazareth, whose motherhouse is located in TACA's territory.

In addition to these routine educational activities for its own members, TACA has provided workshops to benefit all the church workers of the area. On March 24, 1974, for example, it sponsored a day-long exploration of the theology of mission. One hundred twenty-five people from 23 parishes and ten organizations attended. Several months later TACA members, with a little outside help, embarked on a continuing program to provide orientation to those church workers who were entering the rural ministry for the first time. In odd-numbered years, this orientation consists simply in introducing them and giving them some general background information at a regular TACA meeting. A major effort is made during the even-numbered years, when the Council designs and stages an entire day of learning sessions for new people. These sessions center on the church and civic resources that are available and on rural psychology.

A large majority of those who have been assigned to TACA's territory within the past two years participated in the latest orientation day, August 29, 1976. They were able to meet one another and many of the more experienced rural ministers. They also heard valuable talks on, among other things, rural geography, mission ministry, vocations, rural culture, pastoral counseling, rural health and the programs of local social service agencies.

The resolution which TACA adopted in June of 1973 when it reorganized itself had stated that the Council would foster the growth of its members along social, spiritual and intellectual lines. As we have just seen, the intellectual side of things was well taken care of and spiritual development was continually encouraged by the worship services which, by a natural process, had become an increasingly important feature of each meeting.

But what of social growth? Practically from the beginning, TACA's meetings had included a meal, so there was always the opportunity for the members to chat informally and become better acquainted. Moreover, the June meeting each year had been primarily social in character, a kind of party to kick off TACA's summer recess. In 1974, the Council took steps to develop its social program further. Twice during the summer, it sponsored picnics for its members. This practice has been continued with picnics in succeeding years. TACA's people have reacted enthusiastically to these "play days" and they have contributed significantly to building up a very human sense of community within the organization.

So much for the Council's support activities. Since 1974, it has also fulfilled its new advisory role and done so with considerable effectiveness. TACA's immediate success in this line of work will seem less surprising if we recall that the organization had been active already for three years. It did not truly represent the rural part of the archdiocese in the sense that a large percentage of the rural Church workers were members. Nevertheless, over the years TACA had come to be thought of in Louisville and in convents and rectories throughout the area as the voice of the nonmetropolitan counties. Because the Council was the only Church organization that identified itself as rural, others assumed that its opinions were typical of rural opinion at large. So, when it officially began to advise the archdiocese on questions related to the rural area, the grounds for acceptance of its recommendations had already been laid. It seemed natural to everyone that TACA should be speaking out.

An organization can tender advice on its own initiative or in response to a request. The advice that the Council dispenses on its own is given through its committees and through the various liaison people it has placed with archdiocesan bodies. Much of the work of the liaison people is quite informal. Sometimes their advisory role is as simple as making the members of a diocesan agency aware that the rural area exists. They advise, in effect, that the agency consider the whole archdiocese when making decisions that will affect the whole archdiocese. On one occasion, two TACA representatives reported that they had found it necessary to "educate" the members of one commission. The members were debating a resolution on all Catholic schools after having gathered data only on the schools in Jefferson county where Louisville is located!

The more formal work of giving unsolicited advice has been carried by the committees. The work of two of them is of special interest. TACA's leadership had long felt that there was a great need in the rural area for more and better family counseling. The Research Committee on Family Relations was established to discover whether this feeling was justified and, if so, to make recommendations on ways of solving the problem. Pursuing its mandate, the committee administered a survey in March, 1974 to 41 priests and a number of sisters and Protestant ministers, striving for a representative geographical mix. As expected, the need for help in family counseling was confirmed. Early in May, the committee contacted the Archdiocesan Family Relations Center and submitted its proposal for establishing a rural area counseling program. There was no response and in October TACA's board of directors, acting through Father Williams, took up the issue. Father wrote several times to the Center and conferred with Archbishop McDonough on counseling, but as the year ended no resolution had been reached.

More time passed without a break in the official silence, and it began to appear that the recommendation was dead. Perhaps it was, as far as its specific terms were concerned. But the idea of providing some kind of counseling services for the rural counties had been firmly planted and it persisted, provoking discussion in Louisville, making its own way slowly. Finally the announcement came: the Family Relations Center would set up a branch office in Nazareth. Such an office was duly established and in operation by mid-November 1975. The committee's work, bolstered by the objective evidence of need elicited by its survey, had borne fruit.

By far the most dramatic piece of advice the Council has produced, perhaps its most dramatic accomplishment of any kind to date, was the project of the Personnel Policies Committee, which is made up of five of the seven members of the board of directors. On February 5, 1974, the committee submitted a report on rural ministry to the archbishop. Some 30 pages in length, it contained sections on "General Suggestions for Personnel Placement," "Mission as Ministry in the Archdiocese of Louisville," "Proposals for More Effective Ministry in Rural/Mission Areas," and "The Role of Religious in Rural/Mission Ministry." An advisor, reviewing the booklet for the archbishop, called it one of the most challenging reports that had ever been produced in the archdiocese.

The same advisor also noted that TACA's leaders would have to be patient in waiting for their recommendations to be acted on, and this prediction proved true. The only formal result of the report so far has been the appointment of three non-voting "rural consultants" to the personnel commission. Once again, however, TACA had planted an idea, one that would have wide-ranging consequences. The report on personnel policies distinguishes between rural counties and mission counties (those where the Catholic presence is slight or nonexistent) and identifies the primary needs of the two sections. With respect to the mission counties, it suggests devoting a greater share of archdiocesan resources to missionary activities and, more specifically, seeing to it that each county has at least one resident priest.

This distinction, with the accompanying emphasis on the need for upgraded services in those areas where the Church was least well established, might have faded and been forgotten if TACA had not pursued it further. When a year went by without a satisfactory response on the archdiocesan level, the board of directors arranged a meeting with the Personnel Commission to reinforce the recommendations that had been offered. At that time a very specific and detailed plan for clustering parishes and redistributing church workers within the archdiocese was proposed.

This plan has never been adopted, but one of the guiding principles behind it has. Through a process that began late in 1975 and presumably is not yet complete, ministry in the mission counties is being restructured. One new parish has been opened and additional personnel have been assigned to a series of interlocking teams so that nearly all the counties are presently being served by both priests and sisters. In the long run, the effects of this initiative upon the archdiocesan Church could be profound. TACA cannot claim sole credit for it, but clearly provided very valuable leadership by generating precise, creative recommendations and by urging their adoption with patience and persistence.

Besides offering such unsolicited advice (and perhaps partly as a result of this activity), the Council has attained the status of an organization whose opinion is actively sought. In February of 1974, Archbishop McDonough wrote to ask TACA's president, Father Williams, to attend a meeting aimed at developing an archdiocesan policy on the role of Catholic schools in integration in Louisville. Father was made a member of the Archdiocesan Planning Board some months later, and by the end of the year, TACA had been completely accepted as a major church organization. Now, on virtually every occasion where the archbishop seeks broad-based advice before making a decision, the Council is among the groups called upon to give their views.

TACA's leadership was very happy to see this development and for good reason. A group giving unsolicited advice normally exists to recommend change and reform to those in authority. Such a group, then, is by nature in an adversary position with respect to the authority, at least part of the time. The board of directors had been aware that there were elements of an adversary relationship in TACA's dealings with the archdiocese. Some considered the organization belligerent, self-righteous, troublesome. When Church officials began to ask for the Council's opinion on various matters, however, it underlined the fact that TACA was part of and subordinate to the archdiocese. Formal acceptance as a consultant was good in itself. It also meant that TACA could promote rural causes with less danger of provoking a negative reaction. Because the Council was seen as a trusted and sensible ally, "one of us," the fact that it sometimes encouraged reform would not seem so threatening.

Looking back over TACA's history, how shall we sum it up? TACA is one of the largest Catholic rural area ministry organizations in the United States. And it has done nearly everything an area ministry organization can do—provide several kinds of support, advise in three different ways and run its own apostolic programs. It has survived the loss of its founder, two major reorganizations, and storm and strife in plenty. In the process, TACA has proved that priests and sisters can labor side by side extremely effectively, that the principle of voluntary cooperation can work on a large scale, that a great deal of good can be done with slender resources.

TACA does have a few problems. For one thing, it has operated since the beginning on an extremely small budget. Each member pays five dollars per year in dues, and this is the Council's total revenue. There is some feeling that additional sources of funds should be sought so that the organization can expand its activities. The leaders do not want to ask the archdiocese for money for fear TACA will lose its independence, but they are beginning to explore other possibilities such as grants. Second, as in most volunteer organizations, the bulk of the actual work is carried out by a relatively small band of individuals who rotate from sitting on the board of directors to serving as chairmen of committees to taking on special assignments. After almost six years, these faithful few are tiring and something must be done to get a larger percentage of the membership to participate actively.

More importantly from a ministerial point of view, the Council has been unable to move significantly beyond a concern for the nurture of Catholics. As we have noted, an Ecumenical Committee was created when TACA moved into its third phase. This body planned and administered a survey, as did two other of the organization's committees when preparing for advisory action. Within a year, however, the effort lost momentum and the survey data was never put to effective use. TACA's regular meeting in March 1975 was designed as an afternoon of interdenominational prayer and discussion, and about a dozen non-Catholic ministers did attend. But that has been the extent of the Council's ecumenical activities. Every so often the suggestion is made that membership in TACA be thrown open to non-Catholics as a way of adding an ecumenical dimension to its work. However, so far no general support has emerged for such a change.

The Council has a built-in interest in evangelization of the unchurched, since a significant number of its members minister in those mission counties singled out for attention in the recommendations of the Personnel Policies Committee. This interest obviously influenced the deliberations of the committee. It also prompted the adoption of evangelization of the unchurched as the topic for discussion at TACA's meeting in December 1974. But when a few members subsequently proposed that task forces be set up to take some action on evangelization, no volunteers stepped forward and the idea was quickly dropped. The failure of this attempt to come to grips with the issue provoked some controversy. The priests of the mission counties began to question whether TACA, most of whose members serve in those rural areas where the Catholic population is relatively high, was really sensitive to their concerns. A possible split in the organization was avoided, however, and the missionaries continue to work within TACA, hoping to stimulate more attention to the needs of the unchurched.

This matter of establishing task forces leads to a consideration of the last of TACA's prominent problems. Despite the rather complex evolution of the organization, the membership is still not unanimous on what range of tasks it ought to be undertaking. There are still voices that cry out for the resumption of apostolic programs, for the conversion of TACA from an advisory group back to an action group. In fact, in an unofficial way, the change may be said already to have taken place. The Council now serves as a channeling agency to place people in rural ministry. Participating parishes send job descriptions to TACA, and the Council then notifies religious communities of these openings. Though it does not represent a conscious change of policy, this is clearly an action program, a function that is different in kind from the activities the organization has pursued these past few years.

Is TACA on the verge of a fourth phase, then? That seems unlikely. In January 1976, a consultant was called in to moderate a discussion of whether the organization's structure should be altered to permit direct apostolic action. After much debate, the members decided against such a move, concluding that TACA had found its niche. Those who wanted to initiate action could do so by forming independent task forces which, though they might be made up entirely of TACA members, would remain separate from the Council. In view of this apparent consensus, it appears that the one action program presently in operation is merely an anomaly. It may be abandoned in time or, quite possibly, spun off as the work of the first of the contemplated task forces.

TACA's problems are real, but none of them is the sort that breaks organizations or renders them ineffective. At present, it has about 70 active members. Its leadership is capable, creative and experienced; Father Williams was elected to a second two-year term in November 1975. In spite of its miniscule budget of $350 a year, the organization does its job rather efficiently. In spite of the disagreement over structure, it operates almost serenely, as though after years of crisis and turmoil, it had merged with the gently rolling Kentucky landscape and breathed in the mild atmosphere. There is a sense that TACA should be where it is.

Ironically, the Council won its way to this state of peace by a miscalculation. The area councils that diverted TACA from its purpose and caused it to become a support and advisory group never materialized. They remained a mere proposal, a shadow.

This turn of events proved in the long run to have benefitted the Council, though it cut short a promising beginning. The members were forced to go on searching for a ministry that was right for them, one that took realistic account of the organization's limitations, one that contented the majority and still allowed freedom of action to those who were not content. Having identified this congenial ministry, the men and women of TACA can look forward to a stable and productive future.

3. The Support Emphasis

*The Northeast Texas Clergy-Religious Group
in the Diocese of Dallas*

On the third Thursday of each month, with relatively few exceptions, Bishop Thomas Tschoepe of Dallas gets into his car and goes to a meeting. There is certainly nothing very startling about this; the bishop attends meetings often enough. But these particular gatherings are unusual for several reasons. First, they are not held at diocesan headquarters but at various parishes and institutions scattered to the north and east of Dallas, some of them in very small towns. Second, the subject of the meetings is never diocesan administrative affairs, and they do not require extensive preparation. Third, although he participates in the meetings, the bishop does not have to solve any problems, hear any formal complaints or make any weighty decisions. Altogether, as meetings go, they are quite a pleasant change.

They are a pleasant change for many people—for parish priests both religious and diocesan, for sisters working in schools and hospitals or employed as pastoral assistants, for permanent deacons and their wives, for laymen like the editor of the diocesan newspaper. At last count, 91 people were receiving invitations to the meetings and about 50 were actually gathering on a typical Thursday. Getting there is usually neither easy nor convenient; most members have to drive considerable distances after putting in a full day's work. The fact that they keep coming year after year indicates that the organization which sponsors the meetings is offering them a service they value.

The name of this organization is the Northeast Texas Clergy-Religious Group (NTCRG). It is not a particularly appropriate title. As just noted, lay church workers are admitted to membership, so the qualification "clergy-religious" does not hold. In addition, while most of the members live and work in northeast Texas, a few come from southwest Arkansas and southern Oklahoma. Imprecisely named or not, however, the group is thriving. It provides support for the church workers who make it up, and does so very effectively.

Pure support groups of an informal type are common enough in church circles. Catholic priests, for example, often meet regularly on the deanery or vicariate level for shared prayer and fellowship. In an ecumenical context, most county ministerial associations are support-oriented. But these organizations tend to be small and are composed exclusively of professional peers. The Northeast Texas Clergy-Religious Group is extraordinary because of its size and because it mixes people from different occupations within the ecclesiastical world in a support relationship.

Large, heterogeneous support groups are rare simply because a great many church people are fundamentally action-oriented. In any support organization, sooner or later the discussion of ministerial problems will spark a desire to attack those problems. When a group is small, this desire may come to nothing because of lack of leadership or a lack of concrete ideas on how to proceed. As the size and the diversity of the membership increases, however, so does the probability that both ideas and leadership will be available. A dynamic is set in motion, and the support organization turns into an action organization through a process that is often painful and divisive.

How has NTCRG succeeded in remaining a pure support organization, then? It is partly a matter of physical distance. The group serves a territory that measures about 200 miles east to west and about 100 miles north to south. This has tended to discourage cooperative efforts except among neighboring parishes. But while distance is a contributing factor, it is not the only nor even the most important cause. The disadvantages of distance can be greatly reduced by intelligent program selection and design. NTCRG is a support group today primarily because the members want it that way. They have agreed to pursue their direct ministry in other ways, preserving NTCRG's identity as an organization which serves the needs of the ministers themselves.

This conscious decision has made all the difference. The transformation into an action group that overtakes many larger support organizations often, perhaps usually, results from the fact that the members have no clear idea where they want their organization to go, what they want it to be. It starts as a support group only because that is the easiest place to start, and evolves as circumstances and the activist tendencies of the members dictate. This drifting process can be easily controlled. Simply by articulating and discussing the purpose of their organization, the members of NTCRG have made that purpose firm. NTCRG can become an action group only by choice, not by accident.

However conscious of the nature of their organization the members are now, there was not much precise planning at the founding of NTCRG. It was almost an afterthought. After 25 years in parishes outside his home town of Texarkana, Father Robert Johnson was assigned a post in that city in 1968. He took over as pastor of Sacred Heart Parish from another priest who had retired but who continued to live in the rectory as pastor emeritus. Two years later, the older priest marked the thirtieth anniversary of his ordination, and Father Johnson decided to arrange a celebration for him. The nearest parish to Texarkana within the diocese is 65 miles away, the next nearest is 80. So when Father Johnson began assembling a guest list, he soon found that he had to range far afield. He persevered, nevertheless, and succeeded in gathering 35 priests and sisters from all parts of the diocese. The celebration, which consisted essentially of a meal and a liturgy, was held on May 1, 1970.

Part of the way through the festivities, an idea began to circulate through the rectory. Why not meet again, just for the sake of meeting? It was not necessary to wait for a special occasion. Father Edward Haggerty volunteered his parish in Jefferson as a meeting place and the decision was made. No one present was quite aware of it at the time, but the Northeast Texas Clergy-Religious Group had just been born.

The second meeting of the newly formed group added a new element. To the liturgy and meal was joined a presentation/ discussion period. This is the format that NTCRG meetings have followed ever since. The group gathers about 5:00 p.m. on the appointed day each month (except for June, July and August, which are kept clear for summer vacations). The first item on the agenda is a social hour and this is immediately followed by a meal, composed usually of dishes brought in by the people of the host parish. At 6:45 or 7:00, a speaker gives his views on a particular topic, and at the conclusion of his talk the floor is thrown open for discussion. Depending on how central the meeting place is, discussion will end between 8:00 and 8:30, and the meeting closes with a concelebrated Mass. Sometimes this liturgy is held for the group alone, while on other occasions parishioners are invited to attend.

This describes the sum total of NTCRG's activities involving the full membership. For more than six years, the organization has concentrated on providing fellowship, an arena for the free exchange of ideas, occasions for common prayer and educational opportunities for its people. In a diocese like Dallas, where the Catholic population hovers around five percent of the total and Catholic institutions are scattered and isolated, it is meeting a definite need. The pastoral interest of Bishop Tschoepe in the group—he attends about 90% of the meetings, often driving well over 100 miles to do so—testifies to that. So does the fact that the organization has grown greatly not only in membership but also in area served. Originally, NTCRG was a northeast Texas organization exclusively. But religious who were transferred to those parts of Oklahoma and Arkansas that were still within driving distance have remained faithful, thus accounting for the interdiocesan character of the group.

When the organization was first formed, it had nothing at all in the way of structure. There were no officers, no committees, no board of directors, not even an official list of members. Father Johnson acted as leader of the group, but his leadership was completely informal. He was not elected to serve, because there was no provision for holding elections; he was not assigned any tasks, because there were no channels for assigning tasks. NTCRG was the most casual operation imaginable.

But little needed to be done to keep the group functioning, and one person's services proved more than adequate. Father Johnson determined a meeting place and a speaker for each month's gathering. Since the members were scattered over so large an area, he initiated the practice of "floating" the meeting place from one parish or institution to another. It was not so much a rotating selection as a random one; the group came together each month wherever Father received an invitation. Lining up the speakers for each meeting tested Father Johnson's ingenuity and powers of persuasion, but he managed to put together a series of interesting programs. Among the topics presented and discussed during NTCRG's first year of operation were the need for Church unity, the Vatican II Constitution on Divine Revelation and the prayer life of the individual.

At the June 1971 meeting, discussion consisted of an informal evaluation of the group's experience. It was clearly unfair to expect one man to do all the work, so the members drew up a list of suggested topics for 1971-72 and expressed the feeling that a committee should be established to handle program arrangements. There was no structure within which to appoint such a committee, however, and a year slipped by before volunteers could be found to sit on it. Meanwhile, Father Johnson conducted business as usual, finding speakers to make presentations on, among other things, the role of women in the Church, the pastoral care of the sick, religious education and the Catechetical Directory, the person of Jesus Christ and the sacraments of initiation. The selection of meeting places was becoming more routinized by now. Four of the year's gatherings were held at a centrally located parish, and the others were distributed throughout different parts of the diocese.

The program committee was finally assembled during the summer of 1972, with Father Johnson as chairman. Topics for each meeting were selected from a list to which the full membership had contributed. The committee did its job faithfully, but when the year was evaluated in May 1973, some discontent with the quality of the meetings was expressed. The programs were inconsistent, it was said. Some presentations were excellent and provoked intense discussion, while others were lifeless. Most of the liturgies proved satisfactory, but a few showed a lack of forethought. Finally, since the meetings were not planned as units, the themes of the presentations and the themes of the liturgies did not match, so that in the course of an evening the group was talking about one thing and praying about something else.

In order to cure these deficiencies, the program committee changed its way of operating. The committee members became more aggressive in seeking outside speakers. They also pressed members to take a turn on the podium if they had special competence in a subject of interest to the group. In addition, they unified each meeting by recommending a Mass, a set of readings and a homily theme that were consonant with the topic the speaker would treat. For example, early in 1974 the group heard a talk on celibacy from Father Richard Smith, S.J. of St. Louis University. This presentation was complemented by a Mass for vocations of priests and religious and a homily that focussed on the idea "I Give Myself to God and His People." The meeting in October 1975 was a Bicentennial celebration, with a Mass designed especially for the occasion. The effect of these changes has been to lend an air of greater seriousness and precision to the meetings, which in turn influences those who are responsible either for the talk or the liturgy to prepare more carefully. The system has won general acceptance and, in spite of some backsliding with respect to liturgy coordination in 1975, is still in force today.

The growth in the role of the program committee is the primary development that NTCRG has undergone. There have been a few other changes, but they have been minor. The program committee itself, for example, is now composed of priests, sisters and a deacon; originally, it seated priests only. None of these adjustments have affected the organization in any fundamental way. Except for the quality of its services and the coherence of its membership, NTCRG is largely the same in 1976 as it was in 1970.

Since more often than not change comes as a result of crisis, the natural conclusion to draw from the organization's stability is that it has faced few serious difficulties. This is true. Because of the enthusiastic support of the bishop and other officials, the group has been accepted within the diocese. Internally, it has suffered from a tendency on the part of the majority to leave all the work to a few and the lack of money to hire outside speakers has caused difficulties. NTCRG members do not pay dues, so all expenses must come from the treasuries of the parishes and institutions of the area, and there is no fixed budget. But these problems have not amounted to more than a source of occasional annoyance. At the organization's present level of operation, so little work and money are needed to run NTCRG that neither inactivity by the bulk of the membership nor financial uncertainty is a threat to its basic health.

If the support that NTCRG offers its people is not much affected by organizational problems, it is severely limited by circumstances. The members are engaged in many different kinds of work, which means that they have many different schedules. As a result, it was impossible to decide upon a meeting time that would please everyone, and the third Thursday is merely the most acceptable compromise. Trying to serve a clientele spread over 21,000 square miles also has inherent difficulties. The group cannot meet very often or for very long, because people have to spend so much time on the road. These conditions place definite restrictions on NTCRG's activities. There would be no point in attempting to provide in-depth educational opportunities, for example, on the basis of four hours' contact time a month.

Granted that the services NTCRG provides are limited, they are also very solid. For the past six years, the members of the organization have had a place where they could go to lay aside the responsibilities of office for a short time and just be themselves. Moreover, the meetings have permitted them to evolve a network of personal and professional contacts within the diocese. They have become less isolated, and that is the touchstone of success for any support organization. Life for the clergy in rural rectories, for the religious in city schools, for church workers of every sort, has grown a bit more comfortable and more pleasant since NTCRG became a fixture in northeast Texas.

There is also the educational aspect of the organization. The talks and discussions featured in each meeting are a source of information and intellectual stimulation that would be hard to replace. Some topics, like "Contemporary Trends in Christology" (November 1973), have enabled the members to update their knowledge of subjects with which they were already familiar. Others, like "The Charismatic Renewal" (December 1971) or "The Rite of Reconciliation" (January 1976) have presented new material that has deepened their understanding of the modern Church. In either case, the members profit from being part of an inquiring, interested group of people.

In Father Johnson's view, the principal significance of NTCRG is as "a sign of unity" to the Catholic Church in the diocese. The fact that a good percentage of the clergy and religious regularly communicate and worship together has fostered a spirit of respect, trust and friendship among those who work in the apostolate. At a general meeting in 1971, the members of NTCRG agreed that the ultimate goal of the organization should be to build Christian community among the church workers it serves. They have made important strides toward achieving this high but elusive ideal.

4. The Advisory Emphasis

*The Deanery Three Council
of the Diocese of Tulsa*

In December of 1972, the diocese that covered all of Oklahoma was split into the Archdiocese of Oklahoma City and the Diocese of Tulsa. The new ordinary of Tulsa, Bishop Bernard Ganter, was eager to develop a diocesan pastoral council and he promptly took steps toward that goal. On June 21, 1973, he divided the diocese into seven deaneries and during the summer clerical and lay delegates from those deaneries met to draw up a set of proposals for the pastoral council. This committee recommended, among other things, the establishment of deanery councils to act as a bridge between parish and diocese.

These changes eventually produced the desired diocesan council. But they also had another effect which the bishop and his advisers had not foreseen. In the southeastern part of the state, a diocesan priest, Father Donald Brooks, had been actively promoting area ministry since 1969. At the time the Diocese of Tulsa was formed, Father Brooks was head of an action organization called the Southeast Oklahoma Multicounty Project (SEO) which covered 22 counties. It was floundering badly. The members had carefully planned a series of apostolic programs, but the organization was so unwieldy they were beginning to doubt if they would ever be able to implement them.

The recommendation on deanery councils led Father Brooks to examine his position. A deanery council was at least as good a potential instrument for area ministry as SEO was and had the added advantage of being part of the established order. The way was open to tie the notion of interparish area cooperation more closely to the official diocesan structure. Father Brooks was elected dean of Deanery Three in September of 1973 and, with characteristic energy, moved decisively in a new direction. He began to think in terms of a council for Deanery Three (Haskell, Hughes, Latimer, LeFlore, McIntosh and Pittsburg Counties) that would function as an area ministry organization.

SEO faded away shortly thereafter, but it left a legacy to those who would serve on the deanery council. In its four years of life, the group had created and fostered a spirit of cooperation among the local clergy. Though it did so imperfectly, it had also promoted the essential habit of thinking in area terms. Most importantly, SEO trained the future leaders of the council, convincing them that cooperative planning was a precise and demanding task. When they had to plan in their new organization, they were ready.

Deanery Three Council was formed on December 2, 1973. The committee working on the diocesan pastoral council had requested that the pastors and parish councils of the deaneries meet and pass along their ideas. During Deanery Three's meeting, Father Brooks simply asked those present if they would like to continue coming together on a regular basis. The response was overwhelmingly positive.

He immediately began working out a goal and a structure for the group. He reviewed SEO's experience and sought the advice of various consultants, asking himself this question: "Given the particular circumstances of this particular diocese at this particular time, what is the most valuable service an area organization can perform?" The answer he came to, in simplest terms, was "Advisory ministry." Clearly there was need for a middle-level organization within the diocesan framework whose overall task would be to project a coherent vision of ministry. This vision, if carefully communicated downward to the parishes and upward to the diocese, could stimulate united action on many fronts.

Guided by this concept, he designed an advisory organization that would surface ministerial needs, produce practical plans for addressing these needs and urge that the plans be implemented. It would operate no direct action programs itself. It would merely provide a perspective, an idea and a plan which others could adopt and act on. Besides performing this advisory function, its primary reason for being, the group would offer some support services, consisting mostly in maintaining good communications among the parishes and between parishes and diocese.

All this planning led to the drawing up of a model for the Council which the members promptly accepted. That model has remained essentially unchanged, receiving final form in a constitution adopted in 1976. (See Appendix B.) The Council concerns itself with all aspects of the Church's mission: pastoral care, ecumenism, evangelism and social ministry. Moreover, its membership reflects the entire local Church, being composed of the pastor of each parish and two lay delegates from each parish and mission. (Professional parish staff people are also invited to join, but they do not enjoy voting privileges.) These delegates speak not for themselves but for the institutions they represent, emphasizing that Deanery Three Council is the middle level in the diocesan pyramid.

Being part of the structure of the Diocese of Tulsa, the Council enjoys a form of moral backing that many area ministry organizations lack: it is a mandated body. In practice, the member institutions cooperate freely. But the fact remains that the group is a recognized diocesan organization, one in which the bishop expects all the parishes and missions of the deanery to take part. In the same way, Deanery Three Council is a representative body, since it brings together delegates from each Catholic congregation in its service area, and in turn sends delegates to the diocesan pastoral council. These two qualities lend its decisions and initiatives a certain legitimacy that no unofficial group could hope to claim.

There are five parishes and seven missions in the six counties that make up Deanery Three, and these units can generate a total of 29 delegates for each meeting. In fact, however, some of the missions are too small to place two people in office, and the Council functions with an average, consistent attendance of about 20. It meets every two months on Sunday afternoon for three hours. Each meeting opens and closes with prayer and consists primarily of a presentation on some topic of general interest, various reports and discussion of the advisory project currently before the Council.

The organization is set up quite simply, thanks in great part to the memory of SEO, which evolved a structure so complex that the members were paralyzed by it. Deanery Three's constitution provides basically for control by the assembly component of the organization. There are no standing committees other than an executive committee whose actions are subject to review by the assembly. Moreover, the duties of the president are simply to conduct meetings and to serve on any *ad hoc* committees that the assembly may appoint. Finally, while the dean serves on the executive committee and appoints the treasurer, the offices of president and vice-president may be filled by others.

The Council has carefully resisted the temptation to multiply organizational components. Provision is made in the constitution for one staff position, an executive secretary. This job has always been handled by a volunteer, a member of the group, so it has not represented a structural elaboration. There have been no task forces and, up until now, there have never been more than three committees in operation at any one time.

In the beginning, Deanery Three Council lacked a stable financial base. Father Brooks paid all the organization's expenses for paper, duplicating, postage and so forth out of his own pocket, as he served both as president and executive secretary of the group. Starting January 1, 1975, a more equitable system based on congregational subsidies was adopted. Each institution pays an amount to the Council determined by its income, ranging from nearly $400 for the largest parish to $3.50 for the smallest mission. These assessments added up in the last fiscal year to a budget of $840, which proved to be ample for funding the group's activities.

Deanery Three Council is quite a new organization and so, when speaking of its accomplishments, the proper question to ask is not "What has it done?" but rather "What has it done so far?" After a period spent in getting organized, the Council settled down and went to work. Its ministry has been divided rather unevenly between support activities and advisory activities.

Support has consisted in simple fellowship among the members, in continuing education and in communications. The communications have taken several forms. The dean and the diocesan pastoral council delegates act as channels through which information from the parishes of the deanery passes upward to the bishop and his staff. At the same time, the Council routinely receives information from the diocese and passes it along to the parishes, and provides an opportunity for one parish of the deanery to make announcements to the others. In March of 1975, for example, the Council was told of a plan whereby needy parishes could borrow from parishes with a surplus, and one pastor invited the members to his parish for a talk on the new Catechetical Directory. More recently, a chancery official came to ask for the members' suggestions on recruiting a full-time diocesan youth director. The pastors also exchanged ideas about sponsoring Vietnamese refugees.

The Council has not placed a great deal of emphasis on continuing education. At various times during the past two years, the members have heard presentations from the director of Catholic Social Services, the diocesan director of communications and the priest in charge of introducing the new rite of reconciliation. And materials on parish restructuring drawn from recommendations made by the U.S. Catholic Bishops' Advisory Council have been discussed. But nothing approaching a consistent educational program has been attempted.

As noted earlier, the Council has spent the bulk of its time surfacing ideas for ministry, making plans for apostolic programs and urging their implementation. Sometimes it need take only the first of these steps to stimulate action. At its meeting on March 31, 1974, for example, the question of launching a deanery newsletter came up. As a result of the ensuing discussion, two members, one priest and one layman, got together on their own and started the paper. Relying on local businesses for support and on local talent for reporting and writing, the two men created an attractive, professional four-page publication. *Good News*, which appeared monthly, was an improvement on the average newsletter in a number of ways. It was printed rather than duplicated. The editors inserted a green masthead and a sprinkling of green headlines for color and contrast. And the articles themselves, ranging in subject from a history of local parishes to diocesan news to a highly specific "what's happening" column, were well-written and interesting. The newsletter terminated after eight months because the diocese began publishing a paper of its own, but while it lasted it was an impressive piece of work.

Deanery Three invested minimal time and energy in the newsletter. An hour or so of discussion and its part was done. It has also carried out three other projects, however, and these have required a great deal more exertion. In mid-1974, a planning process was designed that allowed the organization to make formal, carefully-considered recommendations to those in a position to implement them. Its major projects have all grown out of this process.

Three steps were involved. First, at a retreat meeting of the Council, the primary ministerial needs of the deanery were to be listed, and a few were to be selected for attention during the coming year. Next, an action plan was to be constructed for each of the problem areas that had been singled out. This plan would open with a statement of need which explained why action was called for; its reasoning would be supported by interviews, statistical data, church documents and so on. Then would follow a detailed outline of a practical apostolic program. The third and final step in the process would be to devise an effective way to approach the appropriate persons and groups and persuade them to carry out the ministry the Council was recommending.

Deanery Three Council adopted this process at its meeting on July 14, 1974 and has followed it faithfully. The planned retreat meeting to list the needs of the deanery was held on August 18. By September 15, the members had agreed to focus on three problem areas: adult religious formation, evangelization and the media, and lay ministry. Working drafts of the papers on formation and evangelization were ready shortly after the end of the year and went through a series of revisions. Finally, in May, the Council completed action on the plans for all three ministries.

The document which relates to the question of lay ministry will serve to illustrate how Deanery Three's advisory instruments turned out in practice. The statement of need outlines the history of Catholic Action groups, quotes generously from Vatican II's *Decree on the Laity* and *Constitution on the Church*, and concludes that the role of lay people in the Church demands immediate expansion to correct past neglect. This serves as introduction to a two-page action plan. Here certain measures are recommended to the parishes, the diocese and the deanery itself.

The parish receives the major emphasis. Each parish council, the plan suggests, should identify and evaluate the lay ministries currently in operation. A lay ministry action group should then be set up to reinforce existing ministries and stimulate new apostolates involving lay participation. Once these steps have been taken, each parish should undertake a spiritual renewal aimed at sensitizing the laity to their proper role. A specific timetable for carrying out these tasks is offered.

For the deanery level, the plan envisions a commission on the ministry of the laity that would help the parishes work through all phases of the program just described. This commission would remain in existence for two years and then yield its functions to a diocesan body which would become the permanent coordinator for lay ministry in the diocese. According to the plan, a new department within Catholic Social Services might take on this responsibility.

The final section of the document, which is supposed to present a scheme for getting the group's recommendations accepted, adds up to little more than a supplement to the action plan. It says only that the parish councils must exercise leadership within their own territories and select people to serve on the deanery commission, that the deanery commission must prepare itself to support the parish action groups and that, for the time being at least, the diocese should merely be kept advised of progress at the lower levels. Nowhere does it specify what course the members of Deanery Three Council should take to persuade people to act.

The documents on adult religious formation and evangelization are also weak when it comes to articulating a strategy. Nevertheless, the Council began to press its recommendations as soon as they were formulated. The dean wrote to the bishop in June 1975, calling attention to the three areas in which the Council was interested and asking for support. Then the delegates took summaries of all the advisory materials to their respective parish councils. They explained their plans and encouraged the councils to start working on the ministry that seemed most crucial to them. Three decided to focus on evangelization and a fourth chose lay ministry.

Meanwhile, the Council had appointed committees to review the documents. Their reports suggested several important refinements, which were adopted late in July 1975. Since the changes all relate to the action plans, they presumably represent dissatisfaction with the quality of these plans. There was good cause for this dissatisfaction, if the reactions of the diocese and the parishes are any indication. It has been some time since the final touches were put on the advisory documents in all three areas of concern. A deanery commission on evangelization was set up in the fall of 1975 which produced, among other things, a hand-out explaining how news releases on parish events should be written up for local papers. But aside from this, very little has happened.

Like any advisory organization, Deanery Three exists to make recommendations. Whether or not these recommendations are implemented, however, depends on circumstances beyond its control. A suggested program might conflict with other advice that the diocese receives, for example, or be disrupted by the unexpected transfer of a particular pastor. Nevertheless, it is clear that the advisory organization has a responsibility to develop plans that are as practical as possible and urge their acceptance as persuasively as possible. To do anything else is to invite frustration.

The members of Deanery Three Council recognize this responsibility and accept the fact that they have not completely fulfilled it. Morale suffered when their recommendations failed to provoke much response. One person even suggested that the organization abandon the advisory approach. The Council is displaying a healthy cohesiveness, however. It recently completed action on a formal constitution which reaffirms the philosophy on which it was founded. Moreover, the members have committed themselves to starting over and running through the planning process again in hope of turning out recommendations that will be more readily acceptable. In spite of some reservations, there is no talk of quitting.

Nor should there be. As we have seen, Deanery Three Council is a young organization, and the three sets of recommendations it has produced are its maiden efforts. By surfacing the need for action in adult religious formation, evangelization and lay ministry, the people of the Council have demonstrated that they can project the vision which loomed so large in their original plans. If they can now succeed in catching others up in this vision so that it begins to color reality, they will have a marked effect on pastoral ministry in the diocese.

5. Social Ecumenism in Action

*The Interchurch Coordinating Council
of West-Central Missouri*

Reverend John Bush, the United Presbyterian minister who helped found the Interchurch Coordinating Council and served for five years as its executive director, says that the most remarkable fact about ICC is that it ever got started in the first place. The section of west-central Missouri known as the Kaysinger Basin is not an especially promising place in which to launch an ecumenical area ministry organization, especially one concerned with social action. This is country strongly influenced by conservative evangelicalism, and although religion is extremely important to the people, they are not used to thinking in ecumenical terms. Moreover, the feeling is widespread that religion pertains primarily to personal conversion and has no right to meddle in secular affairs. A person goes to church to worship the Creator, not to listen to a sermon on other people's problems.

Nevertheless, in this uncongenial setting, ICC was born and flourished. Early in 1967, the staff of the United Presbyterian Grand River Parish, Rev. James Bullard, Rev. John Newell and Mr. John Robinson, drew up a proposal for an ecumenical action agency serving a low-income area near the Kansas-Missouri border. These men had noted the success of such urban ministry groups as the Metropolitan Interchurch Agency in Kansas City. If cooperative social ministry would work in the cities, they felt, there was no reason why it could not work in the country, and so they adapted the urban models and began to seek support for their venture.

Through Presbyterian sources, funds were obtained for a person to serve part-time on the staff of the Grand River Parish and part-time in developing the new organization. In October, Reverend Bush arrived from Kansas to accept this job. Meanwhile, the originators of the proposal had put out feelers to a number of denominations to see if they were interested in participating, and on January 5, 1968 an exploratory meeting of denominational representatives was held. By March a prospectus for the new group had been drawn up, including a statement of purpose and plans for funding. Attached to this prospectus were religious statistics for the seven counties ICC planned to cover: Bates, Vernon, Henry, St. Clair, Cedar, Benton and Hickory. When a set of working guidelines was adopted on June 3, 1968, ICC was solidly in business. (For text of the constitution and bylaws that were eventually adopted see Appendix B.)

The charter members of the group were the local judicatories of eight denominations: United Presbyterian, United Methodist, Cumberland Presbyterian, Catholic, United Church of Christ, Reorganized Church of Jesus Christ of Latter-Day Saints, Disciples of Christ, and Missouri Synod Lutheran. Since then the Latter-Day Saints and the Missouri Synod Lutherans have withdrawn and the Protestant Episcopal Church, the American Lutheran Church and the Presbyterian Church in the United States have joined. ICC was and is funded by contributions from the judicatories. During 1968 the United Presbyterian Church carried the entire financial burden alone, but then a system was devised whereby each participating judicatory would commit itself annually to a given sum. This system has not worked perfectly, but it has functioned well enough to provide ICC's basic operating expenses through the years.

The Council's structure is highly appropriate to an ecumenical action group. It follows a consortium model rather than a conciliar one. The conciliar organization operates by consensus; all or most of its members must agree on a certain objective and on the means of achieving it before action can be taken. Without minimizing its advantages, this approach has several major drawbacks. Forging a majority agreement, for example, often involves delay. More to the point, it usually involves compromise. The conciliar model is best for a group of like-minded people who have relatively little trouble reaching consensus. It can paralyze an organization whose members work from different sets of assumptions.

The consortium, on the other hand, takes diversity into account. It is a loose confederation which has no power to bind its members to act. The usefulness of this approach for an ecumenical agency will be obvious. A number of denominations might see the value of banding together for social action. But, given their different theological orientations, they might strongly disagree on what problems to address and how to address them. They would hardly want to be in a position where majority vote could force an unacceptable ministry on them.

ICC is so organized that all the participating denominations need agree on is the general value of social ministry. In its own name, the group does nothing but surface problems that call for action. If two or more members have an interest in actually dealing with a given problem, the organization stimulates the formation of a task force to carry out the work. Although it retains close ties with ICC, this task force is technically an independent body. Thus, the member denominations are not identified with it. This structural arrangement gives the denominations the opportunity to cooperate in ministry, but allows them to choose the level and frequency of this cooperation.

From the beginning, ICC had four components: cabinet, assembly, task forces and staff. The cabinet, which met monthly, was made up of representatives of the sponsoring judicatories. It was the decision-making body of the organization, conducting day-to-day business, making policy and drawing up the budget. But its most important duty was to identify and define ministerial needs, and to stimulate the emergence of task forces to meet these needs. It also certified task forces as eligible for services from ICC's central staff. An executive committee of officers handled routine business between cabinet meetings.

The assembly, which met twice a year, was advisory to the cabinet. Its members were supposed to voice the concerns of their Churches and review the programs of the Council, offering their evaluation and suggestions. As a body of delegates from local congregations, the assembly was designed to complement the cabinet, which represented the denominational leadership. By combining the two viewpoints, the founders of ICC hoped to make the process of surfacing needs thorough and effective.

ICC's action arm consisted of groups of volunteers who were

interested enough in a particular issue to do something about it. These task forces could and usually did receive support from the staff but, as noted, they operated their programs independently. While the cabinet and the assembly were parts of the Council like cells in a body, the task forces were like children in a family, reliant to a degree on their parents but clearly separate beings. Moreover, again like children, they were expected to mature to the point where they no longer needed staff services and began operating completely on their own. The Council could then start the cycle anew by certifying task forces to address additional needs.

At the start, there were only two staff positions: executive director and secretary. Three others were added over the years, as the multiplication of task forces demanded a corresponding growth in staff services. The duties of the director included running ICC's office, doing research on area needs and representing the organization in dealings with other church bodies. He also had major responsibilities with respect to the task forces, serving as an *ex officio* member of all these groups and helping them accomplish their goals.

We saw that ICC was formally in existence by June 1968. But because the director was only part-time at that point and the organization's structure had to be worked out and denominational support secured, the Council did not really become operational for some months. Its first public activity was the spring assembly of April 1969. This event was attended by 102 people from eight denominations and four secular groups and focussed on identifying those issues that were of most concern to the participants.

There were two issues that the assembly did not have to surface, because they were already very prominent. As is the case with most organizations, the impulse to create ICC was not entirely theoretical. There were perfectly practical circumstances that cried out for the formation of such a body. The first of these circumstances was the federal government's announced plan to build a large dam and lake in the Kaysinger Basin. This was sure to have a tremendous impact on the economic future of the area, and some planning was required to prepare the people for what lay ahead. At the same time, the Basin faced a serious strip mining problem. For years a major company had been gouging the earth, leaving it scarred and ugly. A few groups had taken preliminary steps toward advocating legislative controls, but much more needed to be done. The founders of ICC made these problem areas their first targets and in the summer of 1969 the task force on the Kaysinger Project and the task force on land reclamation were set in motion.

Once this start had been made, activity picked up rapidly. In September the organization issued a brochure announcing that the cabinet had approved the formation of nine task forces and was soliciting members for them. Two of these task forces fell by the wayside, but seven were still active as the year ended. Included were a task group on education for ecumenism, which tried to arrange ecumenical prayer services and living room dialogues; on hunger, which aimed at getting a food commodity program established in each of the seven counties; on the Kaysinger Project, which focussed on keeping the public informed of the dam's progress; on Montrose Lake, which concentrated on ministry to visitors to a local resort; on land reclamation, which merged with other groups to lobby for legislative change; on youth concerns, which worked to find employment for young people; and on mass communications, which busied itself collecting information on religious materials that the media had used or could use. Clearly, 1969 was a year of promise for the young organization. Operating on a tiny budget of $13,000, the founders managed to stimulate ecumenical cooperation and the first stirrings of action on an impressive number of fronts.

If 1969 was a year of promise, 1970 was a year of growth. The organization established its routine and worked hard to become an accepted and effective force in the seven-county area. Of the means the Council adopted to accomplish this, none was more successful than the strategy of freely cooperating with other agencies. It developed especially close working relationships with the University of Missouri Extension Service, the West-Central Missouri Rural Development Corporation (the local OEO community action group) and the Kaysinger Basin Regional Planning Commission, inviting each of them to send liaison people to sit in on cabinet meetings. The boundaries of ICC's territory had been drawn so as to coincide with those of the regional planning commission. For this reason, the two agencies had a special community of interest and in the fall of 1970 they moved in together, sharing office space and clerical staff on the square in Clinton.

Although ICC's first assembly had drawn 102 people, the second drew only 48. Attendance picked up again in 1970, but it soon became evident that something was wrong. The semi-annual meetings were not giving effective advice to the cabinet and no new ideas for ministry were emanating from them. In the fall of 1970, the Council turned away from the notion of a single assembly for the whole Basin and set up a series of "mini-assemblies" in four different locations. This did not work either, and in the spring of 1971 the general meeting was resumed. From this time on, however, faith in the assembly concept was on the wane.

In spite of this problem, ICC matured as an action-oriented organization during 1970. The task force on the Kaysinger Project became inactive because construction of the dam was delayed, but eight new task groups were founded and most of them flourished. Three of the eight were concerned with specifically church matters. The task force on counseling and pastoral care set up a program whereby clergymen received training in counseling from staff at the area mental hospital. The task force on church planning sponsored a consultation in November of 1970 that was attended by 38 people from eight denominations. And the Stockton Lake Ministries Council focussed on providing opportunities for worship and Christian fellowship to vacationers.

The other five groups were concerned with social problems. Two were formed in the usual way: a problem was surfaced in the cabinet, volunteers were recruited by cabinet members and staff, and the task force was organized with staff help. The establishment of a state junior college in the Basin was the goal of the task force on education. Meanwhile, a housing group explored several alternatives for providing decent housing for the poor and elderly, including seeking funds to start a housing development of its own.

The last three social action groups originated outside ICC. The Bates County Cooperative Ministry was a parallel development, sponsored by the Christian, Methodist, Holiness, United Presbyterian, Baptist, Catholic and American Lutheran Churches to address a single county's special needs. In 1970, this ministry became affiliated with ICC so as to have access to the larger organization's resources and staff. It operated like a mini-ICC, a "county working unit" as it was called, setting up task forces to function in such fields as youth activities, day care centers and help for the mentally handicapped.

In the fall of 1970, the local community action agency received an OEO grant to set up a Mobilization of Resources project in west-central Missouri. Such a project would involve providing staff to develop and put to use various kinds of resources in a ten-county area. One aspect of this general program gained a more or less separate identity. Called Crosslines, it consisted in a network of volunteers who engaged in face-to-face social action. Shortly after it received this grant, the agency contracted with ICC to administer the funds and ICC accordingly began work on both Mobilization of Resources and Crosslines. Four new staff people were hired to run these programs, which were launched with great optimism.

These were ICC's new operations, and they help to explain why 1970 was a year of growth. But some of the older task forces played a significant part, too. The group concerned with hunger succeeded in persuading the Department of Agriculture to set up food commodity programs in the four ICC counties that did not have them already. The members then turned their attention to training in nutrition for those who received the food. The land reclamation task force had helped instigate the creation of a state-wide Coalition for Preservation of the Good Earth, and this group had drafted a strong strip mining bill to be introduced in the Missouri Legislature. Finally, the task force on youth concerns had set up a labor pool that had provided part-time jobs for about 100 young people during the summer months.

As 1970 ended, 12 task forces were active, thanks to the efforts of some 300 people. In the next three years, the Council simply built upon this solid base. There were no radical changes in administrative policies or personnel. The Council went on forming new task forces and sustaining those already in existence. It was a stable time, a time for enjoying the successes and learning from the failures. Between 1970 and 1973, ICC became more than an experiment. It evolved into an established fact.

No condensation of the Council's activities in these years could possibly be very clear. There were simply too many activities. About 20 task forces were in operation at one time or another. Some worked steadily for the entire three years, while others flicked in and out of active life. To complicate matters still further, the larger task forces took on a number of jobs in succession, went up blind alleys and had to turn back, changed plans, adjusted, revised. Rather than follow all these tangled lines, we will simply review some of the high and low points of ICC's career during the period.

The organization's outstanding achievement between 1970 and 1973 was the success of the task force on land reclamation. In April 1971, the Missouri Legislature passed the strip mining bill which this group had helped sponsor. Most of the benefits that an organization like the Council obtains for the citizens in its area are either small-scale or temporary or both. That is an inevitable result of working with very limited resources. But the strip mining bill was important, and the effects of its passage were clear, immediate and permanent. In this matter ICC had done the Kaysinger Basin a great service.

After the legislature acted, the land reclamation task force turned in new directions. It began to advocate the restoration of the 30,000 Missouri acres that strip mining had devastated. Working through the regional planning commission, the group obtained a grant to demonstrate how reclamation of mined land could actually be accomplished. Then, in 1972, it severed its ties with ICC and set out on its own. It thus became one of the two task forces which have completed the cycle envisioned in the original plans for ICC and become entirely independent of staff services.

Three other task forces incorporated as separate organizations, but all of them continued afterward to rely on the ICC staff for aid and guidance. The first of these, the one on housing, failed due to circumstances beyond its control. As noted above, the group originated in the usual fashion late in 1970. Six months afterward, it established itself as the Concerned Housing Group, Inc. A long search for direction and focus culminated in a decision to buy a piece of land and develop a low-income housing complex. By April of 1972, a building site had been purchased with money made available through the United Presbyterian Fund for the Self-Development of People. The task force applied to the government for a construction grant and continued planning in the expectation of receiving it. At that time, however, federal housing programs were being cut back and the members were told that no funds were available. Staff people went to Washington and lodged a protest, but all to no avail. Finally, in September of 1973, the group sold its land and gave up the struggle.

The task force on human relations, which incorporated in 1971 as Rural Action, fared better. Funded by the Mobilization of Resources grant mentioned earlier, Rural Action attempted to combat poverty and racism by forming local chapters of such organizations as NAACP and Welfare Rights. Within a three-month span, it solicited 6000 signatures protesting the demise of the federal commodities distribution program, managed to win some concessions from the Clinton Housing Authority on the way a public housing unit was being managed and brought enough pressure to bear on this agency that it voluntarily adjusted its policies on racial segregation. In addition, it organized the black community in Clinton to agitate for extension of sewer lines into the black section. But Rural Action, like many organizations engaged in highly controversial activities, did not have a long life. By the fall of 1971 it was no longer in existence.

We have already seen how the task force on counseling and pastoral care was founded in 1970 to offer training to area clergy. Shortly after this, the group dropped its emphasis on pastoral matters, shortened its name to the "task force on counseling" and turned its attention to providing trained secular counselors for the people of the Basin. In August of 1971, the task force received a $10,000 grant from the Missouri Division of Mental Health to set up a counseling center. This was accomplished in early 1972. By April the center was offering some limited services through an agreement with Human Behavior Associates of Joplin. The agreement expired in July, but by then the task force, strengthened by a renewal of its grant from the state mental health agency, had stabilized and established its identity. A second change of name seemed appropriate, and so the task force on counseling became Community Counseling Consultants.

The members of the retitled group, five clergymen, a doctor, a lawyer and the principal of Clinton High School, became the board of governors of the counseling center and soon had it in independent operation. On February 8, 1973, Reverend Bush reported to the cabinet that the center had hired a clinical psychologist and the chaplain at the local mental health hospital to work 12 hours a week each. This service was continued through the end of the year and beyond, as the center became a fixture in the basin.

Generally speaking, the two federally-funded projects that had begun in 1970, Crosslines and Mobilization of Resources, did not perform exceptionally well. This is not to say that they did no good at all; Crosslines in particular involved a large number of ordinary citizens in a variety of useful works. The results, however, did not match the expectations that the original OEO grant of $62,000 had aroused. There are, no doubt, many reasons for this, but one factor in particular stands out. The projects required some active cooperation between ICC and the West-Central Missouri Rural Development Corporation. The corporation had a different perspective on volunteers and social action than that which motivated the denominations sponsoring ICC. As a result, conflicts developed that slowed down and disrupted the operation.

Those connected with the Mobilization of Resources project made a gallant effort to bring together local people and organizations, coordinate their activities and give them technical assistance on administration, application for grants and the like. It did not work, however; what Mobilization of Resources had to offer was simply not enough. When the funding ran out on August 31, 1972, the staff disbanded, proud of their efforts, but disappointed in the effects those efforts had produced.

Crosslines was slow in developing, primarily because of delays in recruiting staff. By March of 1971, however, Crosslines organizations had been established in seven of the ten target counties and the enlistment of volunteers was under way. December saw the publication of the first issue of the project's newsletter, *Crossing Point*; activities at this time included transportation for the elderly, a reading group for the blind, and providing Christmas presents for hospital patients. Because the work being done was spotty and some county Crosslines groups existed only on paper, a decision was made soon after to concentrate energy and resources. Margo Holm, Crosslines director, reported to the ICC cabinet on February 17, 1972 that she would give up the attempt to start any more local units and concentrate instead on developing the four or five operations that seemed to have taken firm root.

Between February and August 1972, Crosslines ran a number of programs: emergency "hot lines" were established and a directory of public-interest organizations in the area was compiled. The most successful venture was a transportation service that helped elderly, isolated and/or handicapped people get to hospitals, pick up commodity foods and so on. This program handled 89 requests in February and 117 in March. In spite of these accomplishments, however, the county units never gained much momentum, and they were unable to carry on independently after the grant money was exhausted.

The period 1971-1973 saw the flourishing of many projects and task groups in addition to the few we have discussed. Some, like the task force on Key '73, survived only briefly, Others achieved moderate results. The task force on hunger, for example, served as coordinator for individuals and organizations interested in the hunger issue, recruited volunteers to help out at county food distribution centers, and testified at hearings in favor of retaining the commodity programs. The Interseminary Project sponsored a course on rural ministry in January 1972 for 17 students from Baptist, Methodist, Nazarene, and Catholic seminaries. Finally, the task force on welfare and human dignity operated throughout most of 1973. Its basic function was to provide information on matters related to welfare and this it did well, distributing at one point 3500 copies of a paper on certain limitations of welfare benefits.

We can conclude this account of ICC's activities in 1971-1973 by glancing at three groups that enjoyed extended lives. The Bates County Cooperative Ministry continued its affiliation with ICC, operating partly as a county unit of the larger organization and partly as an independent body. In its first capacity, the ministry set up local task forces to serve ICC task forces operating in certain fields. The local task force on hunger, for example, took care of Bates County for the ICC task force on hunger. As an independent

agency, the ministry ran thrift clothing stores, assisted with summer camps for youth, helped start a child development center,
acted as sponsor for a "sheltered workshop" at which the mentally
handicapped could learn skills, served as a forum for focusing
community concerns, and more. It was quite active, uncovering
many needs and dealing with them effectively.

Another prominent task group in ICC history has been the
Church Planning Commission. Established on January 19, 1971,
the commission's principal purpose was to foster communication
among local leaders of the member denominations. It seems to
have succeeded in this regard. Attendance at meetings remained
consistently high, indicating that they provided an effective forum
for discussion.

A second function of the commission was to oversee and coordinate the ministries to summer vacationers at Stockton and Pomme
de Terre Lakes. The program began quietly. In 1972 some few
people faithfully attended the scheduled services, but the workers
could not make much of an impression on the mass of vacationers.
The next year was better. Every Saturday morning a "Children's
Funtime," involving crafts and games, was held. On Saturday
evenings there was singing around campfires and a movie. And on
Sunday there were ecumenical worship services at four locations
on each lake. The commission evaluated the effort in August of
1973 and, although a few problems were noted, it was clear that the
lake ministry was growing and was fulfilling real needs. A total of
4000 people were served by 324 volunteers and 13 paid staff that
summer.

The task force on the environment appeared on the scene in late
1971. The members saw their first duty as educational; they concentrated on informing people about environmental issues and
about legislation that would have an ecological impact. After a
time, the group began publishing a newsletter, *Environmental
News Flash*, in order to extend its influence. Then, in November of
1972, the role of the task force was expanded to include direct
action. A plan for establishing recycling centers in each of the
seven ICC counties was drawn up. A year later three such centers
were actually in operation and the largest of them had already
processed and shipped almost 75 tons of paper and metal. The

News Flash for November, 1973 commented with pride—tinged perhaps with a little surprise—on the quick success of this recycling program.

Without a doubt, the period 1971-1973 had witnessed many accomplishments. On budgets that ranged from $17,800 in 1971 to $24,500 in 1973, ICC had initiated program upon program, and helped raise almost $200,000 in grants to support task force activities. At one point during these years, the Council requested an outside agency to evaluate its operation. The evaluation report was generally very positive, asserting that the experiment in ministry which ICC represented had proved successful.

The Council had problems, of course. The same report that praised its record made no fewer than 51 recommendations for improvement, some of which have since been adopted. The major problem areas the report identified were these: a narrow financial base, an unbalanced relationship between volunteers and staff, and a rather loose structure that made planning and policy-making difficult.

ICC's financial difficulties were chronic throughout the period. On several occasions, it became necessary to ask for advances from one of the participating judicatories in order to meet pressing obligations. The problem was not one of management. It was simply that the Council never developed close relationships with some judicatories and therefore did not rank very high among the funding priorities of these bodies. In 1973, eight religious groups belonged to ICC. But of the $17,000 the organization received in subsidies, almost $14,000 came from Presbyterian and Methodist sources; no other denomination gave more than $1100. Moreover, support from the judicatories took the form of contributions which varied year by year. There was no stable system of assessments guaranteeing long-range financial security. The Council always had to function in an atmosphere of uncertainty, dependent for its existence upon sponsors whose commitments were not spelled out.

The second problem was the staff's tendency to take too much responsibility for the work of the organization. According to its constitution, ICC was to seek broad participation in its ministry. One avenue through which local people could become involved, the assembly, never quite caught on. The other avenue was the task forces and, as we have seen, a great many of them were created. But the staff did not place much stress on recruiting members for these groups. The report notes the success of large and active task forces like those on land reclamation and on hunger. It also notes, however, that some were composed solely of a chairman and ICC's executive director.

Virtually all the task forces, large and small, depended heavily on the staff for ideas, planning, administrative services, bookkeeping and help in obtaining funds. In the early life of each task force, this support was essential. No volunteer organization, especially if it is located in a rural area, is likely to have many members with management skills. If it wishes to pursue a sophisticated and wide-ranging ministry, it must obtain professional staff to provide practical leadership.

As we have seen, however, ICC's long-range goal was to give the members of the task forces enough training and experience so that they could eventually split off and work on their own. In only two cases did this happen. All the other task forces remained dependent. Although ICC was a volunteer group, little attention was given to developing volunteer leadership. By 1973, it was becoming clear that staff held most of the responsibility within the organization.

Organizational looseness, the third problem, manifested itself in several ways. The functions of the executive committee were vaguely defined. Although the cabinet technically had the right of review over all actions of the committee, in fact many cabinet members did not know what the committee did nor how it functioned. There was little communication between the cabinet and the task forces. Finally, there was no uniform policy for dealing with the task forces. Because all that was needed for the creation of a task force was the verbal support of the cabinet, and no limits were placed on the number of groups that could be in existence at any one time, they tended to proliferate without reference to any overall purpose.

Perhaps the most important results of this lack of precision were a relative loss in efficiency and a relative incapacity for long-range planning and policy-making. Since task forces could emerge almost spontaneously and the cabinet had no clear overview of their activities, it was difficult to look into the future and aim ICC toward a defined set of goals. The looseness of the structure helped generate a tendency to drift, a tendency visible in the speed with which task forces sprang into life, operated or failed to operate, and died to make room for still others.

These were some of the prominent difficulties that surfaced before 1973. At the end of that year, an event took place that created one more problem. Reverend Bush resigned to become executive director of the Kentucky Council of Churches. An extremely dynamic and capable man, Reverend Bush had moved mountains to bring ICC into existence, and was more responsible than any other individual for its general prosperity. His loss was a serious blow.

Rev. Eugene Moll, moderator of the cabinet, took over as interim director and an intensive search for a permanent replacement was launched. A new man was found and duly appointed soon thereafter, but unfortunately he fell ill almost immediately and could not continue. The post remained vacant until May 1, 1975, when Rev. Lawrence Gill, a Presbyterian clergyman from Kansas City, was hired on a part-time basis. The effect of this 16-month vacancy was considerable. Operations did not come to a halt, certainly; there were nearly as many active task groups in 1974 and 1975 as there were in 1972 and 1973. But the pace was slower. Without the drive that an executive director could supply, ICC moved with less assurance and got less done. Since Reverend Gill took over, the organization has begun to gather momentum again, witnessed by the fact that two new task forces have been created, an old one has been reactivated and the assembly, which was suspended in 1973, has been revived in a new form.

One of the Council's most successful projects got its start in the summer and fall of 1973 just before Reverend Bush left. In June the cabinet voted to accept administration of a federal grant to set up a Retired Senior Volunteer Program (RSVP). The idea behind RSVP is roughly the same as the idea behind Crosslines—face-to-face social action by volunteers—except that the volunteers who do the work in RSVP must be past the age of 60. Mary Frances Clary, long-time ICC secretary, was named RSVP director in August and by September the program was established and on the move.

The recruitment of volunteers and formation of county committees went slowly at first. In the first part of 1974, the program was active in only two counties and there were about 25 volunteers. By June, however, the number of volunteers had jumped to 66 and RSVP began to grow. In the three-month period from June through August the volunteers contributed 2100 hours of work; in the succeeding three-month period, they gave 4400 hours. At year's end the director could report that 144 volunteers were busy in four counties. a growth in ten months of almost 600 percent. The activities in which these retired men and women engaged were many and varied, including such services as working in nursing homes, day care centers and Head Start programs; visiting and helping the sick or home-bound; and keeping in contact with isolated senior citizens through an effort known as Telephone Reassurance. There were, altogether, 23 ways in which RSVP volunteers could make themselves useful in the Kaysinger Basin.

People have responded to RSVP with much more enthusiasm than they displayed for the Crosslines project, perhaps because ICC became better known and more widely accepted in the interval. The program has recently been re-funded for $40,000, following Mrs. Clary's report that in 1975, 242 volunteers had given some 37,000 hours of work, more than triple the total for the previous year. RSVP shows no signs of having peaked and the high median age in the Basin favors its further growth.

Community Counseling Consultants has expanded substantially since 1973 and it is now virtually independent of ICC. In June of 1974, the organization received grants from the Missouri Division of Mental Health to hire two counselors, one for problems related to alcohol and the other for problems related to drug abuse. These, plus another full-time and several part-time counselors, serve the people of four county seats. Fees are charged according to the patient's ability to pay, and they provide about 40 percent of operating costs. The rest comes from state grants and local funds.

The pace of CCC's growth has accelerated recently; from January to June 1976 the client load increased 230 percent. It has also enlarged the scope of its activities to include public education, sponsoring a dinner in March of 1976 at which 146 people heard a speaker on drug abuse among the young. CCC is not a particularly dramatic organization, but it is solid and stable, qualities that have won it the people's continuing respect.

After four years as a forum for ecumenical discussion, the Church Planning Commission disbanded early in 1975.The thrust of its work was not entirely lost, however. The denominational representatives who made up its membership were immediately offered seats in the cabinet, there to continue their efforts to improve interchurch understanding and cooperation. Moreover, the ministry to summer campers that the commission had sponsored was taken over by a task force created especially for the purpose. That ministry had continued in 1974 with roughly the same format as in 1973, serving about 3000 people. A new feature was added to the program in 1975. Three seminarians from different denominations were recruited to circulate among the campers, listen to their concerns and be of help in any way possible. These "campground chaplains" were received so warmly and did such an effective job the idea was retained in the 1976 program and has a firm place in the task force's plans for the future.

The Church Planning Commission had also been involved in co-sponsoring a Matrix program in Bates County. Matrix is a three-day workshop in which the participants study the life of their own community and reflect on it from a theological perspective. The program was originally scheduled for April of 1975, but was cancelled due to lack of interest. After the commission disbanded, a new task force arose that rescheduled Bates County Matrix and vigorously promoted it. On January 17, 1976, a shortened and simplified version of the workshop was held. The 28 people who attended found it a worthwhile experience, and the groundwork is presently being laid for similar workshops in other communities.

In October 1974, an article in ICC's newsletter suggested that a task group on the nation's bicentennial be set up. Its object would be to develop projects emphasizing the contribution of religion to American life. Two months later, such a group was actually established with a small grant from the state arm of the National Endowment for the Humanities. Plans were laid for an educational program, and on three successive weekends in April 1975, a well-attended forum was held on the general subject, "Church and

School: Partners in the Past. Will They Be in the Future?" Encouraged by this success, the task force then joined with the Extension Council of St. Clair County to produce a series of panel discussions of county government commencing in February 1976.

The bicentennial task force completed its work soon afterward, just as another ministry was being launched. At its meeting on February 20, 1975, ICC's cabinet certified a task group whose purpose was to start a FISH hot line, a volunteer answering service that takes calls from persons in emergency situations and puts them in contact with individuals or agencies who can help. The necessary arrangements were soon made and the service was established in Clinton in June. The hot line was designed as a pilot project that other area communities could imitate.

The first new ministry ICC has launched since Reverend Gill arrived in the spring of 1975 was not really new, but rather a resurgence of one of the organization's earliest interests. In July, the hunger task force, dormant since late 1972, was reactivated. The members began by asking themselves how those who were eligible for food stamps but had not registered to receive them might be helped to do so. Some useful theory was developed, but no practical way could be found to transport people to the food stamp distribution centers. Meanwhile, seizing an opportunity to bolster the hunger group, ICC co-sponsored a conference on the world food situation in January of 1976. The task force promptly scheduled a series of follow-up conferences, the first of which was held in Bates County in September.

We saw earlier how some of the concerns of the Church Planning Commission were picked up by other groups after its demise. The same dynamics resulted in the creation of the Small Church Committee in August 1975. The group's purpose is to gather data on local rural churches, help them achieve their aims and promote ecumenism among them. Two months after its formation, the committee distributed a questionnaire asking rural pastors to specify the sort of programs they would like to operate if outside help were available. The returns were sparse and the findings inconclusive, revealing that the committee has not solved the problem of effective communication with its would-be clientele.

An effort to serve the churches indirectly has had more definite results. Working primarily through Reverend Gill, the Small Church Committee has moved to strengthen a local ministerial association made up primarily of pastors of rural parishes whose membership varies from 100 to 500. A continuing education program was introduced which consists of bringing in speakers each month to discuss subjects related to the ministry. In May of 1976, the topic was "Women Clergy"; in June, "Alcoholism." A general rise in attendance at association meetings indicates that the program is effective in bringing the priests and ministers together. The hope, of course, is that this intermingling and the educational content of the meetings will inspire ecumenical experimentation.

In the past, ICC has not had a set of priorities to guide it in the creation of task groups, but has simply adopted those ministries that appealed to the members and for which there was a clear call. In 1976, a more formal approach is being tried. The cabinet held a planning and goal-setting meeting in January and developed a list of needs which has formed the basis for the establishment of a task force on the aging. The major activity of this body so far has been co-sponsorship of a June training session for clergy and laity that was attended by 22 persons. Plans are currently underway to conduct workshops of this type for individual counties.

The Council's most recent activity has consisted in helping to implement a program called Mother-to-Mother Ministry. The idea is to team three volunteers from participating congregations with a mother dependent upon public assistance. So far, five women have offered their services, attending an orientation session on September 19, 1976. If all goes according to design, the volunteers will become more sensitive to the problems of welfare recipients, and they in turn, with the volunteers' help, will become more self-sufficient.

Except for the search for a new executive director, relatively little attention has been paid to ICC's internal affairs in the period since 1973. Nevertheless, two changes have been made. A budget committee has been added to the cabinet to keep a closer watch on the organization's financial condition. And the assembly, one of the principal structural elements named in ICC's constitution, was restored in an altered form in 1975.

Originally, the assembly was to be an advisory body to the

cabinet, keeping the cabinet up to date on the attitudes of the membership in general, reviewing and commenting on ICC programs. This concept has been abandoned. The new assembly consists of people who gather for a specified event relating to the work of an ICC task force. The occasion for the spring assembly of 1976, for example, was the world food conference held in support of the task force on hunger. The audience was the assembly and its function was simply to listen and learn, not to advise the cabinet on the material presented. By reinstituting the body with these fundamental changes, ICC's leadership hopes to avoid the problems to which the old assemblies were subject, and at the same time to enlist local support for its ministry.

The Interchurch Coordinating Council is now in its ninth year—a truly venerable age in the new world of area ministry organizations. The problems present in 1973 are still present: narrow financial backing, an unbalanced relationship between staff and volunteers, and structural looseness. But it would be wrong to make too much of them. In fostering a practical, working ecumenism under extremely adverse conditions, the organization has developed a solid base of experience and considerable resilience.

6. Interparish Cooperation

*The Leon Regional Catholic Community
of the Diocese of Des Moines*

The armchair traveler who glances at a map of Iowa will notice that the counties that rim the southern border of the state are precisely square, like children's building blocks. Decatur County rests snugly in the middle of the row, with Wayne to the east and Ringgold to the west. Just to the north of Decatur is Clarke, another square that perches on the bottom row like a blunt tower upon a triple-chambered base. The county seat of Clarke is Osceola, about twenty miles from the county seat of Decatur, which is Leon. The county seat of Wayne is Corydon, some twenty-five miles from Leon. And the county seat of Ringgold is Mt. Ayr, about twenty-five miles from Leon in the opposite direction.

In April of 1971, three priests gathered at Leon to form a team to serve the parishes in all these towns—and the churches in Woodburn, Grand River and Maloy as well. The senior member of the group was Father Paul Connelly, who for the past 14 years had been director of Catholic Charities for the Diocese of Des Moines. He was joined by Father John Lorenz, pastor at Osceola, and Father James McIlhon, pastor at Leon. The four square counties had been designated the Leon Regional Catholic Community, a subdivision of the diocese, and the priests planned to become joint pastors of the 1200 or 1300 Catholics who lived there and at the same time look beyond them to the 32,000 other residents of the area.

The experiment has not worked out precisely as planned. Experiments in ministry rarely do. But after five years and more the Leon area organization—the team of priests plus an area council—is still healthy, gaining in strength of service and depth of support. It differs from most area ministry groups, especially action ones, in that it has led a relatively peaceful life. Area groups often exist in an intermittent state of crisis, financial or operational or otherwise. The Leon ministry has experienced some conflict, but deep crisis of any sort has passed it by.

In part, this stability results from the fact that Leon is a very special kind of area organization. The definition of such groups stipulates that they must operate on a level between parish and diocese. All seven churches in the Leon area retained canonical status as parishes when the team was formed. Their parish councils remained intact, and they continued to worship and to run the bulk of their programs as separate congregations. Therefore, since the team and area council operate on a level between these parishes and the diocese, they meet the definition. At the same time, however, team and council serve as staff and leadership for all seven churches, which resemble a single parish in that they share pastors and are subject to financial assessments levied by a central authority. Moreover, the work of the team priests and the council is almost exclusively parochial in nature, in the sense that nothing they do, whether in nurture of the Catholic community, ecumenism, evangelism or social ministry, varies greatly from what might be done in a highly progressive parish, given the difference in the size of the area served. Even though the Leon group is clearly an area organization, then, it is also in a way a parish writ large, a parish with three pastors, seven congregations and seven councils!

Because the Leon ministry is so intimately bound up with a parish-like structure, it has been invulnerable to many of the pressures that commonly plague area organizations. For one thing, team and area council do not represent a greatly new and unfamiliar organizational form, but rather an extension of an old form, the pastor and parish council. Money, the lack of which has shipwrecked many an area group, has not been a major difficulty either, since the ministry has had a reliable source of supply in the parishioners of the seven congregations. Finally, the specific problems that the group has had to face have been mostly pastoral difficulties with the priests are trained to cope with, and so they have not mushroomed out of control. Many area organizations have been radical experiments. The Leon ministry, while definitely innovative, represents a relatively conservative departure from tradition, and this has worked in its favor.

The framework for a large-scale team effort in the Des Moines diocese has existed since 1969. At that time Bishop Maurice Dingman divided the diocese into 12 "regions," with the strong recommendation that the priests of each of these new subdivisions cooperate pastorally. This action set everyone thinking in area terms. In the next few years a number of ideas were tried in various regions, and one of them was the Leon ministry.

The notion of a rural team first surfaced in the summer of 1970. One of the pastors in the towns around Leon retired and Des Moines, like many another diocese, was short on potential replacements. Father Connelly, who was eager to get back into direct pastoral work after many years as an administrator, was strongly interested in the team concept. He also knew that Fathers Lorenz and McIlhon, the only two priests left in the area, had talked about launching some sort of cooperative effort. Seizing the opportunity, he drew up a proposal for a team ministry, gave it to the two pastors for their approval and then submitted it to Bishop Dingman. The bishop responded to the idea enthusiastically. Among other things, he altered the boundaries of a few of the diocesan regions so that the four counties the priests proposed to serve would constitute a region by themselves. This gave the Leon ministry a definite place within the diocesan structure. His overall strong backing made ironing out the necessary details relatively easy, and by October 1970 the tentative structure and goals of the new organization had been set down on paper.

The team was not initiated immediately, however. All the priests felt that the parishioners of the four counties should have some orientation before a new and significantly different pastoral arrangement was imposed on them. For the next six months they and Bishop Dingman met repeatedly with the people of the parishes, discussing, explaining, getting reactions. Finally, everyone seemed reconciled to the prospect of having a team of priests except for small groups in two parishes. The proposal to form a team was then presented to the diocesan Association of Priests and, when that group approved it unanimously, the final decision to act was made. On April 16, 1971, Bishop Dingman formally announced the appointment of Fathers Connelly, Lorenz and McIlhon as co-pastors of all seven area congregations. The three priests moved into the rectory at Leon and by the end of the month the ministry was functioning. A Regional Council was established in June.

The priests submitted a written report on the state of the ministry in August, and we will review the results of that analysis shortly. Suffice it to say for the moment that the Leon group's first summer was crowded with activity, not all of it highly organized. The Regional Council, which was composed of one lay representative from each parish (in reality, one representative from each parish council), did not know what to do at first and had to grope for an identity. Gradually, however, some fairly clear parameters emerged. The council would handle the routine finances of the ministry as its primary responsibility. It would also serve as a channel of communication from parishes to diocese and vice versa. And it would plan and seek funding for area-wide programs.

The financial duty was the most pressing as well as the most complex one the council had to face. It was decided that the individual parish councils were to keep financial control of whatever applied to that parish alone. If the steeple at St. Bernard's in Osceola needed repair, for example, the Osceola parish council had to pay for the work. If an awards dinner were planned at Immaculate Conception in Maloy, the Maloy council had to fund it. The area council, for its part, was required to take care of the team's living expenses and cover expenses incurred in connection with the area as a whole—office needs, for example, or printing costs for the area bulletin. In order to meet its obligations, the council laid assessments upon the parishes on the basis of the number of envelope holders on each one's rolls. There was some grumbling when the amounts of these assessments were first announced, but all the parish councils cooperated and monthly installments began coming in on schedule. The total area budget for the first year was set at $27,000.

The council took up its other responsibilities with equal quickness and determination. It kept in touch with various diocesan agencies and the bishop's office, so as to be in a position to provide accurate information to the parishes. As far as areawide programs were concerned, the council explored the possibility of hosting a workshop for lectors, applied to the Campaign for Human Development for $500 to defray the cost of a workshop on soil stewardship for ministers and community leaders, and arranged for housing and supporting a group of students from New York who volunteered to conduct a four-week summer Bible school in the county seats.

While the council's operations were an important part of the whole Leon ministry, the heart of the matter was clearly the direct pastoral work of the team priests. The report they drew up in August 1971 indicates the directions that work was taking. The co-pastors put considerable emphasis on their practice of constantly rotating church assignments so that each priest officiated at all seven churches within a three-week period. They felt that providing the people with variety in sermons, pastoral counseling and liturgical style might stimulate them to a more active piety and a better understanding of the post-Vatican II Church. The priests also mention spending a good deal of time visiting the sick, the elderly and shut-ins, planning for programs in religious education, and encouraging the efforts of the various parish councils.

Besides citing some of the services provided for Catholics in 1971, the report lists certain advantages that the community at large had derived from the presence of the team. These include cooperative contacts with Protestant pastors in the four counties and the simple benevolent presence of three priests enthusiastically engaged in a new ministry experiment. The last section of the document speaks of the good relationships among the team members and closes with the hope that more long-range planning can be accomplished in the future.

The activities that occupied the Leon group during its first few months have remained typical of it to the present day. The area council still concerns itself with money matters, with such programs as workshops and vacation Bible schools, and with parish-diocese communications. Despite personnel changes, the team still rotates church assignments, puts stress on home and hospital visiting, keeps ecumenical contacts open, takes an interest in community affairs. New methods, new approaches have been introduced from time to time. For the most part, however, clergy and laity have simply learned to work with increasing sensitivity and competence at the same basic tasks, like a farmer whose skill grows with every passing spring.

Given these circumstances, there is little point in detailing the story of the Leon ministry since 1971. It would be highly repetitious and not very enlightening. Let us focus instead on a review of the mechanics of the organization, exploring how and why it works. Then we can examine some of the more significant ways in which it has pursued its mission.

The clerical team holds the executive and most of the administrative power within the ministry. While it is true that the area council pays the priests' salaries and provides for their upkeep, they are in no sense employees of that body. The co-pastors, as a matter of fact, are *ex officio* members of the council and dominate the discussion process by which it makes decisions. It would be unfair, however, to see this dominance as a deliberate effort to limit lay participation in the organization. The team priests, to a great extent, have had their position thrust upon them. As is typical of small parishes, there are relatively few laymen in the Leon congregations who are willing to serve on church boards. Lay attendance at area council meetings is usually good, but active involvement is minimal. It is inevitable in a situation like this, given the respect in which Catholics have traditionally held their clergy, that the co-pastors would control the ministry by an easy and natural process, whether they wanted to or not.

On the other hand, there is no recognized source of authority within the team itself. The organization does have a formal head, a Regional Coordinator who reports to the bishop on the progress of the ministry. It is understood, however, that this office does not confer any power over the other team members. Moreover, it rotates among the priests. Every four months there is a new coordinator, so that in any given year, all three men hold the post for the same length of time. This arrangement effectively nullifies any special prestige that the office of coordinator might otherwise carry and places the priests on a footing of equality.

The team functions in this democratic spirit. Father Connelly is the most influential member because of his age and because he has been with the ministry since its founding while both his partners are relatively new. (Father Lorenz accepted another assignment in October 1973, and was replaced by Father Lawrence Hoffman; Father McIlhon was replaced by Father Joseph McDonnell in the summer of 1974.) But all decisions affecting the organization are made by consensus, after patient and careful discussion. Each Monday morning the priests meet for three hours to talk about any matters of significance that have arisen in the past week and to plan for the week to come. There is lively give-and-take, the issues at hand receive a thorough airing, and no conclusions are reached unless everyone is in basic agreement.

While this way of operating may seem so egalitarian as to be unstable, it works quite well. The continued success of the team is clear proof that a non-authoritative association of priests can prosper over a long period of time, even in the face of considerable obstacles. The personality differences among team members have in one or two instances been considerable, and the work has been difficult and demanding. Yet this rather free-wheeling system has proved itself equal to all challenges, so much so that the team has not only held together but grown more effective with the passage of time.

It follows from the team's consensus style of operation that the Leon ministry is not highly structured. Structure implies authority and accountability, and this would threaten the delicate balance that sustains the organization. The area council and the team are the only structural components the ministry can boast. The priests work closely with the various parish councils as well, but since these groups do not deal with area-wide concerns they are technically outside the pale.

The priests' daily activities are regulated, of course, by the decisions reached in council meetings and their own team meetings. But they also observe a general division of labor which was set up at the beginning. As has already been noted, church assignments are rotated according to a predetermined pattern in order to expose all the people to all the co-pastors on an equal basis. Each Saturday night and Sunday find Father Hoffman, Father McDonnell and Father Connelly at a different parish from the one he served the week before. Also, each priest takes responsibility for visiting the county hospitals on a schedule tied in with his parish work. Finally, each relates to a specified set of parish councils for a year and a half or two years, then takes on another set. This is as far as the rules extend. For the rest, the priests are masters of their own work schedules.

Originally, the members of the team were to have certain specialties; one would handle religious education, another would involve himself in social concerns and so on. This plan was never adopted in practice. All the priests share roughly the same jobs day in and day out. A typical week for each will include liturgy and sermon preparation, parish and/or area council meetings, ministerial alliance meetings, a prayer group session, home and hospital and nursing home visitation, parish administration work, bulletin preparation, counseling, religious education classes and travel. To reemphasize a point made earlier, this routine does not vary greatly from normal parish routine, except for the last item listed. Because the priests provide services to seven congregations, they are on the road a great deal, each man logging some 3,000 miles per month. This extra travel time, plus the fact that they must think in terms of the religious needs of four counties at once, makes them a new breed, familiar yet different: "area pastors."

In glancing over the history of the Leon organization since 1971, what events, qualities, developments stand out as particularly worthy of note? We have seen that the ministry has moved along free of major crises. But the road has not been entirely smooth. Although the priests have gotten along very well in general, there has been some disagreement among them. Although the area council has done a good job in general, there have been times when it did not function adequately. Most importantly, although the people of the area have generally accepted the team, there has been resistance, and sometimes bitter resistance, to its presence.

Of the churches within the Leon fold, three were parishes before the ministry was founded, three were missions and one, the Corydon Catholic Community, had not yet been formed. The people in Corydon and in the mission churches welcomed the team, because to them it meant increased pastoral services. The people in Leon were also happy with the new arrangement. They had had a resident priest; now they were to have three and would become the center of an area ministry. The only people who were not content were groups in the other two parish churches. They felt that their resident priest was being taken from them and that the services they had always enjoyed would certainly be cut back.

The difficulty in one parish was entangled with family loyalties and, despite some lingering resentment, today the scars are mostly healed. The introduction of the team provoked much more open conflict in the other congregation, where the effects of the struggle have been more marked. Within that congregation, those who preferred the traditional parish setup to the concept of area ministry gained a majority of the seats on the parish council and took vigorous action to defeat the plans that the team and the area council had made. More than once, members of the church formally petitioned Bishop Dingman to terminate the team. The situation gradually became more tense until, early in 1974, several of those on the council publicly refused to lend the parish financial support. When the three priests challenged their position, every council member resigned. After this, the parish remained without a council for more than a year. It never became divorced from the Leon community in any formal way, but in the eyes of some it was an unwilling prisoner of the system.

Elections in May of 1975 brought in a new parish council and there are solid signs that the gap between parish and area ministry is gradually closing. The issue is resolving itself in practice. However, this resolution has been achieved only at the cost of great pain. Looking back, Bishop Dingman and the co-pastors wonder if they should have delayed initiating the ministry until a true consensus was reached within all the parishes.

The question does not admit of an abstract answer. No one would deny the value of consensus in such a situation, and certainly consensus could have been made an absolute prerequisite to the launching of the experiment. The danger, of course, is that this prerequisite might never have been fulfilled. The bishop and the team priests spent six months trying to convince people that the advantages of accepting the team would outweigh the disadvantages, yet groups of parishioners fought hard in resistance to the area plan. Obviously, their reaction was rooted in strongly-held attitudes, some of which were probably unconscious. If consensus had been required, the formation of the team might have been blocked indefinitely. It was necessary to make an administrative choice between two alternatives, either of which could have had unpleasant consequences: on the one hand, possible conflict; on the other, possible frustration of the entire ministerial plan. The decision in Des Moines was to pursue the plan with only a limited consensus and, from an organizational viewpoint, it seems to have worked out well.

But the organizational viewpoint is not the only valid one. Again, those who objected so strenuously to the creation of the team belonged to parishes that lost resident pastors in the transition. It is a rare congregation that does not long to obtain or retain a resident pastor of its own. The constant presence of a pastor stabilizes a church and lends it a solidity it can attain in no other way. Moreover, a resident priest strengthens the identification of a parish with its local community, enabling it to serve more effectively. The creation of an area organization like the Leon ministry represents a gain in efficiency, perhaps, but a loss in terms of the values traditionally associated with the small rural parish. The desire to retain these values works in direct opposition to the establishment of such ministries.

This internecine conflict within the organization caused considerable disturbance. On balance, however, it did not seriously hamper the team priests and the area council in carrying out their duties. We noted earlier that the priests conducted an evaluation in which the impact of the ministry on area Catholics, on the community at large and on the team members themselves was explored. These three categories may be used in reviewing some of the accomplishments of the Leon group.

The overriding benefit that the Catholics have derived from the existence of the area organization is an increase in the quantity and quality of pastoral presence. At first glance, the mathematics of the situation would not seem to support this conclusion. Before the team was formed, there were three priests serving three counties; now there are three priests serving four counties. Nevertheless, all the evidence, both subjective and objective, indicates that the people in the parishes do receive more pastoral attention now than they did before.

How explain this paradox? First, the priests carry on a fraternal rivalry; each man tries to do as much or more for the people than the other team members. This rivalry could easily have a disruptive effect, but given the generally friendly context at Leon it has been healthy and has certainly worked to the advantage of the parishioners. Second, the ministry is innovative, which creates an atmosphere that the priests find highly stimulating. Third, a multiplicity of pastors breeds a multiplicity of pastoral ideas; each Catholic in the Leon community is a potential beneficiary of three viewpoints, three sets of insights, three ways of doing things. Finally and most importantly, the priests are mandated to ignore parish boundaries and may respond to needs throughout the entire area. The greater flexibility of each priest adds up to better services for all the people.

A more complete pastoral presence has meant many things to the seven rural and relatively isolated congregations. As has been mentioned, the team has brought liturgical and theological diversity to the Catholics of the area. If a man does not respond to Father Connelly's way of offering Mass, he can find out which church Father Hoffman is serving on a given Sunday and go there instead. If he is uncomfortable with Father Hoffman's explanation of Christ's presence in the Eucharist, he can ask Father McDonnell for his opinion on that point. Because their pastors constantly expose them to alternative ways of expressing and interpreting the body of Catholic belief, the people are constantly stimulated to be curious about the dynamic life of the Church and to become involved with it.

All the priests who have worked or are working at Leon are creative ministers, and their presence has brought change to the parishes. This evolution has come about largely through teaching, a responsibility that the team has always taken very seriously. The pastors have experimented with religious education since the beginning, seeking an approach that would "draw" people yet at the same time provide solid instruction. For the first two years, Father McIlhon was in charge of the program and it was oriented primarily toward teenagers. The instruction of children was confined to sacramental preparation classes and a vacation Bible school.

A major addition was made for the school year 1973-74. Reasoning that the youngsters' lack of interest in and knowledge of religious matters arose ultimately from conditions in the home, the priests decided to educate the adults to better understand and appreciate the post-Vatican II Church. They conducted classes themselves, and at the same time brought in an outsider to give a course on the sacraments.

This strategy proved fruitful and might have been continued, but the priests learned of something that seemed to them even better suited to their purposes: the family-centered approach to religious education. A program of this sort was instituted in the fall of 1974, with each man teaching weekly classes to groups in the various congregations. The results have been so gratifying that the team is committed to family education for the immediate future at least. Catholic parents have gradually come to recognize that they must be the primary educators of their children in religious matters, and the team feels that this attitude is of the highest value where the parishioners are scattered over so wide an area.

Formal schooling is only one of the means the team priests have used to educate the people. They and the area council frequently sponsor local diocesan-run workshops on such subjects as parish council operations and lay participation in the liturgy. They have gotten a good response encouraging parishioners to undergo intensive spiritual experiences like Cursillo and Teens Encounter Christ. Finally, they have done a great deal of personal teaching. Besides preparing their homilies and the weekly bulletin with great care—both receive attention at team meetings—the pastors in 1974 took the extraordinary step of issuing a joint statement entitled "A Purchased People: A People Set Apart." Here they explained the theology of the sacraments and laid down guidelines for their worthy reception.

All this education has stimulated an evolution in many of the parishioners' religious understanding and practice. The changes have been gradual and they are not dramatic when weighed against the upheavals that have rocked parish life elsewhere in the nation, but their cumulative effect has been substantial. In 1970, participation in congregational singing was weak or non-existent; today it is general. In 1970 many of the parishes had no lectors or song leaders; now such lay ministries are standard. The formality that once characterized anything even remotely connected with the liturgy is breaking down and being replaced by a more open, relaxed approach. The ritual of the sign of peace no longer makes most people uncomfortable. There are coffee and rolls in the rectory at Maloy each Sunday. And in Leon the monthly parish council meeting immediately follows Mass and is accompanied by a pot-luck meal to which the whole parish community is invited. After Father McIlhon was transferred in 1974, he reported back that the Leon congregations were more progressive than the large parish to which he had been sent, thanks to the leadership the team had provided.

Pastoral presence, to be complete, must be felt not only in the church but in the home as well. The team originally set out to visit each of the over 325 Catholic households in the area once each year. This goal was never quite attained because one or another of the priests failed to make his assigned quota regularly, but the team has in general been very faithful in maintaining personal contact with the people. In the first 18 months of the ministry the pastors made roughly a thousand sick calls, and over the years they have more than doubled the number of hospital and nursing home visits they originally projected. In addition, each of them drops in on parish families at least four or five times a month to share a meal, to chat, simply to keep in touch. Far from depersonalizing the relationship between pastor and parishioner, the substitution of a centralized team for a group of isolated resident priests actually seems to have made it closer.

The first priority of the Leon ministry is to unify and serve the seven congregations specifically committed to its care. As a result, the priests and the council concentrate on nurture of the Catholic faithful and do not place as much stress on the other aspects of the Church's mission as some area organizations do. Nevertheless, they have not ignored the non-Catholic population of the territory. They have always worked for the good of the entire community, and this comprehensive thrust has become more pronounced as the organization established itself more and more firmly over the years.

Evangelization of the unchurched receives the least attention. A high percentage of the people in the area parishes had some involvement in the Key '73 program, and in recent years the ministry has sponsored the showing of religious films at the Decatur County fair. Aside from this, there has been little organized activity. By their energy, openness and dedication, the priests give a witness that breaks down anti-Catholic feeling and stimulates a sympathetic interest in the Church. However, they run no programs aimed directly at converting the unchurched.

Both the team and the area council serve the community more actively in the fields of social ministry and ecumenism. As far as the social arena is concerned, the council has sponsored annual rural life workshops, open to all, which deal with the problems and the future of small country communities. An essay contest for young people on soil conservation has been promoted the past two years, and a series of estate planning workshops is being conducted in cooperation with the state Extension office. The ministry has also tried to respond to the fact that the percentage of both poor and elderly in the local population is quite high. Since 1973, the church in Osceola has been used as the site for a meals program for senior citizens. And, in May 1976, the National Council of Churches asked the organization to help assess the need for a campaign to educate local people on federal food programs. This initiative has resulted in plans to set up a tri-county anti-hunger agency.

Finally, the priests have been very active on their own. They have developed special projects over the years. Father Lorenz, for example, was involved quite substantially with Crosslines and such civic organizations as the Rotary Club during his tenure with the team. Nowadays, Father Connelly sits on the Soil Conservation Board, Father Hoffman is a member of the Rathbun Mental Health Board and Father McDonnell works with a citizens' planning group to increase the effectiveness of Extension service programs. Beyond these specific initiatives, of course, the priests play a significant role in the everyday affairs of the area towns, attending ceremonies and sports events, offering aid and advice to local groups when needed, lending a hand in community public-interest or charitable efforts. Much of their social ministry is informal, based more on "being there" than on major planned programs.

The Leon group's ecumenical involvement is no less substantial. All three priests are enthusiastic members of the ministerial alliances in the four counties and they join in union services at stated times during the year. The Corydon parish, moreover, lends financial support to an ecumenical summer ministry to the vacationers at Rathbun Lake, and the team cooperates with various Protestant ministers in serving the local nursing homes and in maintaining a campus center at nearby Graceland College. Some of the Catholic parishes also share physical facilities with neighboring Protestant congregations. The parishes in Grand River and Corydon use Methodist buildings for religious education and regular worship, respectively, while the Christian church provides space for Catholic religious instruction in Mt. Ayr. Over the years, the team has built rapport with Christians of different traditions, a rapport that is reflected in these instances of formal cooperation.

It is difficult to describe the effects the team has had on the lives of the priests themselves because they seem to live together without worrying very much about their interrelationships. They did not undergo any psychological testing beforehand to see if they were compatible, nor have they ever had any professional counseling on how to deal with the problems of community living. They have been told from time to time that grave difficulties must certainly arise if three priests who were used to working alone had to share the same rectory. Their actual experience, however, has never come close to bearing out such theories. Friction there has certainly been, and some misunderstanding at times, but no more than might be expected in a standard family situation. For the five priests who have served at Leon at one time or another, community living has not only never been traumatic. It has not even been troublesome enough to merit special attention.

The priests are unanimous in praising the personal, professional and spiritual support they have received from the team. Their statement of general approval, it is true, carries one major qualification. The pastors have never been able to develop the common prayer life that was originally envisaged for the team. They pray together for about an hour as part of their weekly planning meeting and hold a communal penance service among themselves at intervals. With these exceptions, their prayer is private or involves outside communities; each man belongs to a *Jesu Caritas* priest group.

Leaving this matter of a common prayer life aside, however, it seems clear that the priests do benefit substantially from living and working together. There is much open discussion of the theological background of the team's work, for one thing. This stimulates thinking and increases motivation by clarifying the relationship between that task and the mission of the Church as a whole. Secondly, the priests can and do consult one another on homily preparation, liturgy preparation, counseling problems. If one attends a workshop, his partners profit from it. If one works out a new way to solve an old problem, his partners hear of it. If one learns something about the parishioners' needs and desires, his partners soon possess the same information. Thirdly, because they have continuing close relationships with others, the Leon priests are psychologically closer to their people. The experience gives them an intimate feel for the family context in which nearly all their people live. And finally, having "brothers" to lean on makes the pastoral job, which is essentially a solitary one, less lonely, less pressured, more humanly comfortable.

The future of the Leon ministry seems quite secure. The system of personnel change which the team has adopted—replacing one member at a time instead of terminating the whole group and starting off fresh with another—assures a basic continuity in the organization's operations. Moreover, the bishop and his personnel board allow the members who remain a very strong voice in choosing the replacement for the man who accepts a new assignment elsewhere. The incoming priest knows in general what is expected of him and sets to work with a commitment to function as part of a peer group.

The greatest advantages the organization has, beyond the competence of the co-pastors, are the solid support of the bishop and the fact that it is an official unit of the diocese, with ready access to the central diocesan structure. Each month the area council hears reports from its representatives to major diocesan commissions, and council and team are often consulted when policy decisions are made in Des Moines. This advisory function is only a minor part of the work of the organization; Leon is in essence an action group with very important support features. But it keeps open a channel of communication with powerful forces outside and above the ministry, and these forces are precisely the ones that can guarantee its long-range stability. If the Leon organization is still intact in 1985, it will be largely because the bishop and his staff will have followed its work carefully and lent it their continued backing.

The greatest obstacle the ministry faces now, the greatest obstacle is has always faced, is the single parish orientation that has been traditional in the Church for a millenium. The people are reluctant to identify themselves religiously with a whole area. But slowly, not without pain, attitudes are changing. A shared religious education program, a shared hymnal and shared liturgies such as area-wide confirmation and first Eucharist services and an area-wide anointing of the sick have helped lay the groundwork for a new vision. The extent to which this vision has emerged may be judged by the fact that when one parish found itself in need of funds early in 1975, another parish voluntarily subsidized it for a period of ten months. And, during the summer of 1976, the organization sponsored a picnic and a Mass celebrated by Bishop Dingman that was well-attended by people from all the congregations. The feeling is growing that the Leon Regional Catholic Community can be just that—a community. This is the principal goal of all the work the co-pastors and the area council are doing. They strive to replace a parochial consciousness with an area consciousness, to redefine what the word "us" means to the Catholics of the four square counties.

7. Interfaith Cooperation

The Morgan-Scott Project for Cooperative
Christian Concerns in Eastern Tennessee

Morgan and Scott Counties, which stretch northwest of Knoxville to the Kentucky line, lie in central Appalachia—that vast, green tract of mountain land that is famous for coal mines, folk art and grinding poverty. The counties, each of which has a population of about 14,000, are not prosperous places. In 1970, when the census was taken, the median family income in Morgan County was $5363 as against a national median of $9590. Twenty-seven percent of these families earned so little they fell below the government's official poverty level. The situation is even worse in Scott, which has the questionable distinction of ranking among the 100 poorest counties in the United States. The median family income was only $4172 in 1970 and nearly half the county's families, 42.1 percent, lived in poverty.

Services, even essential ones, are minimal. In 1973, for example, there were only five doctors practicing in Scott county and none at all in Morgan. And it does not look as though the situation will spontaneously improve in the near future. The median educational attainment is between eight and nine years for the citizens of both counties. Moreover, those who have the most education and the most potential, the young, tend to move away when they come of age because there are few jobs to be had at home.

To say that the situation will not spontaneously improve, of course, is not to say that it cannot improve. As a matter of fact, economic and social conditions in Morgan and Scott Counties have grown somewhat better in recent years through the work of an organization that was set in motion partly by design and partly by accident. In the spring of 1972 Rev. Paul Brown, the local United

Methodist district superintendent, and Rev. William Andes, head of the Southeast Conference of the United Church of Christ, got together to discuss a problem. Each had three churches in small mountain towns that were without the services of an ordained minister. Reverend Brown knew of a young man, Rev. Robert Butziger, who was interested in working in the area; on the basis of this information, he and Reverend Andes came to an agreement. Reverend Butziger would act as pastor to the three United Church of Christ congregations. Then, in his spare time, he would work with his own churches and the United Methodist ones in devising social programs related to health, education and economic development. Nothing dramatic in the way of social action was planned—just neighborly cooperation.

From this modest idea grew an area ministry that has gone far beyond anything ever dreamed of by the two administrators. When Reverend Butziger came to Morgan County during the summer of 1972, he immediately began to enlist support for the ecumenical program he had been charged with. Response was favorable. In September, he was able to convene the first meeting of a new organization with one other clergyman and four lay people from the United Methodist and United Church of Christ congregations in attendance. Within two months the group widened its base, taking in a Presbyterian minister and a Catholic layman. By the end of the year it had begun to develop its first two programs, one on day care and one on health. It had also adopted a rather weighty name: the Morgan-Scott Project for Cooperative Christian Concerns. (The organization's bylaws will be found in Appendix B.)

A firm structure for the organization emerged during the same period. The Morgan-Scott Project (MSP) is an action group. At its heart is a council made up of 15 to 20 interested clergy and laity, who serve as more or less formal representatives of their various congregations. The council is the organization's administrative body. It makes policy, does planning, initiates task forces to carry out the programs it adopts, and is responsible for handling ordinary business. Theoretically, the council controls MSP, providing the grassroots participation and leadership that the Project particularly encourages.

In reality, however, it shares power with two other groups. Very shortly after the council first met, a steering committee (later called the Resource Advisory Committee) made up of officials from the denominations which funded MSP was formed. The duties of this committee include securing support for the organization, helping to set goals and serving as a channel of communication between MSP and the judicatories. As the committee's change of title implies, it does not exercise any direct control over the council. The members are generally content to meet every three months, approve the budget, review what the council has done and offer suggestions.It is clear, however, that as holder of the Project's purse strings, the committee is in a position to influence specific decisions if it chooses to do so.

The staff wields power within the Project in a more immediate and personal way. Normally, when an organization made up of volunteers hires professionals, the professionals tend to dominate operations, whether intentionally or not. This is understandable. Having recognized the professionals as specialists, the volunteer members of the group are tempted to defer to them, looking to them for leadership and following their advice.

MSP is fortunate in that several of the non-professional members of the council are very active. This works against staff dominance since actual day-to-day responsibility for operations is widely distributed. Nevertheless, the staff performs some very important functions. Besides Reverend Butziger, the full time executive director, and Jim Romer, a part-time associate director, both of whom have been with MSP from the beginning, there have been over the years a secretary, an administrative assistant, one other associate director and five or six "interns"—people who volunteer to work for the Project for up to a year for room, board and $200 a month. Butziger and Romer are *ex officio* members of all the task forces; the interns are usually assigned to one of them. Staff members do most of the routine work of the Project—organizing, applying for grants, writing letters, persuading people to help, attending endless meetings and weighing endless alternatives. By so doing they affect the council's freedom to govern. If the staff must carry out the council's directions, then clearly the council's directions must be tailored to the staff's abilities and, to some extent at least, to their desires. And, since the staff people also attend council meetings and join in its deliberations, their influence on the conduct of the organization is quite significant.

Of the two remaining structural elements of MSP, one plays a relatively minor role. When attendance at council meetings began to lag in 1974, their frequency was reduced from twice to once a month. This created a problem; there was no longer any way to react quickly to a situation that demanded immediate attention. The council's response was to constitute its four officers an executive committee with power to make emergency decisions between council meetings. The actions of this committee are subject to review by the full council when it next convenes.

The last component of the organization has been mentioned several times already. Although MSP is action-oriented, it does not take action in its own name. Its work is actually carried out by a number of task forces which the council brings into being as the need for them arises. Thus, for example, if a consensus were to emerge in the council that something should be done about education, it would establish a task force to take responsibility for dealing with the problem. Task forces are technically independent of MSP and may incorporate as separate agencies if their members see fit. Even if they choose to do so, however, most of them retain close ties with the parent body. Council members and staff people provide leadership for the concerned citizens who make up the rank and file of the task groups, and their progress is noted and sometimes monitored by the council.

As stated above, MSP is an ecumenical venture supported by a number of church bodies. Altogether, representatives from seven denominations—Southern Baptist, United Methodist, Lutheran, Catholic, United Presbyterian, United Church of Christ and Episcopal—sit on the Resource Advisory Committee. These denominations sponsor the project in the sense that they contribute at least moral support, advice and guidance. Within the group there are four churches that are involved on the financial level as well. The Methodists, the Presbyterians, the Catholics and the United Church of Christ combine to supply about 55 percent of MSP's annual budget, which has increased from $14,000 in 1972 to $95,000 in 1976. Of this $95,000, roughly $38,000 went to cover basic office expenses and salaries, while $57,000 was used to fund apostolic programs.

Besides being subsidized by these churches, the Project obtains public grants from time to time for particular ministries. The rest of the material support it receives comes from groups (mostly congregations) and individuals, both local and non-local. One church especially, the First United Methodist in Oak Ridge, has backed MSP from the start with money, supplies and volunteer help. Over the years, the organization has developed a network of such "partners in mission" throughout the country, and the aid it gets for office and programs from these sources is substantial. In a three-month period in late 1975, for example, gifts were received from 17 religious and secular organizations and 11 individuals in 10 states.

Like many other rural ministry organizations, the Morgan-Scott Project does its work in an uncongenial setting. We have already noted the poverty of the residents and the fact that the majority of the bright and talented youths leave the area upon finishing high school. In addition, it is not uncommon for mountain people to refuse proffered help; tradition opposes the sort of broad-based social action that MSP is set up to perform. Apathy is another problem, the apathy that comes from experience with a class-conscious governmental structure and with do-good schemes in the past that promised much and delivered little. Finally, mountain society in relatively isolated spots like Morgan and Scott Counties is still a closed system to some extent. Not only does everyone know everyone else, but nearly everyone in a given community is related to everyone else by blood or marriage. It is difficult to aid or even to contact an individual without triggering a set of reactions that travel throughout a whole extended family.

Because it had to operate in such a context and because its founders, both volunteer and professional, had to feel their way in the early days, the Project got off to a slow start. The staff did not know where to go to find funding for specific projects. The organization lacked the political and social contacts it needed throughout the two counties to get things done on the local level. There was a chronic shortage of help, and its first major undertaking, an attempt to set up day care centers in three Morgan County towns, was a failure. Three months, even six months after MSP was formed, there was little indication that it would ultimately succeed.

It has succeeded, however. If an observer tried to represent the history of the Project on a graph, the line he drew would go steadily upward. After struggling through its early period, the organization began to gather steam. Of course MSP did not suddenly become an efficient, smooth-running operation. It is not especially efficient even now, due perhaps to a tendency on the part of the leadership to tackle too many projects at once. But it did attain a healthy level of competence within the first year and, considering the size and budget of the organization, its accomplishments have been impressive.

Since its founding, MSP has fielded a total of 14 task forces, each one dedicated to responding to some specific need. One of the Project's principal aims has been to give the people of the mountains practical experience in helping themselves. The task forces, most of which are basically citizens' groups, have done just that. Acting under the professional guidance of the Project staff, the members of the task forces have learned that they can take an unpleasant situation and change it through a liberal investment of hope, patience and hard work.

From one angle, the task force with the best record is the one on summer recreation for youth. This effort, which is funded by Morgan County and the substate development district, was launched in the first summer of MSP's existence and has been renewed with substantial local participation in each succeeding year. The task group was formed when six young people, four of them from outside the area, volunteered to head recreation centers in different towns during the summer of 1973. The core program in each center was arts and crafts such as painting, ceramics, candle-making and soap-making. When creativity was at a low ebb, the youngsters resorted to more physical amusements like sports and games, berry-picking and hiking. At intervals, the clienteles of all the centers joined for field trips. Aided by a van made available by Morristown College, they drove several times to Knoxville and on one occasion ventured as far as the space center at Huntsville, Alabama.

The recreation project followed the same general pattern in 1974. Each participating community or group of communities furnished a center and took a hand in designing and funding a program doctors and partial funding for a clinic under certain conditions. The council set about meeting these conditions. It incorporated as a non-profit organization and, with the help of MSP staff and others, conducted a survey of the county's health needs. Shortly thereafter, the application for a grant was approved by the Health Services Corps and Morgan County officials made available $50,000 in revenue-sharing funds. Two doctors and a medical assistant arrived to open the Wartburg clinic on July 1, 1973. In November, a dentist joined the staff.

The opening of the Morgan County Health Center, as the clinic was called, was a signal achievement, but the Health Council's work was far from done. Toward the latter part of 1973, funding problems developed as a result of a difference of opinion between the council and county officials. This matter was eventually resolved. Then, in March 1974, the staff wrote a grant proposal that netted $12,000 for X-ray equipment from the state, thus upgrading the clinic's services.

It was clear, however, that the Wartburg facility was inadequate to serve all or even most of the people of the area. Spurred perhaps by the proverbial rivalry between rural towns, two successful grassroots efforts were mounted to expand the health program. Citizens of the community of Petros, noting the success of the Wartburg experiment, joined forces with people from Norma and Stoney Fork to establish the Mountain People's Health Coalition, a group that eventually merged with the Morgan County Health Council. In July 1974, they initiated a clinic in Petros. It is staffed by a full-time nurse practitioner and a part-time doctor and pediatrician.

No sooner had the Petros facility opened its doors than a committee in Deer Lodge began laying plans for their own clinic. The Deer Lodge people joined the Morgan County Health Council, too, and in 1974 and 1975 pursued their goal with the aid of the fund-raising skills of the MSP staff. The Tennessee Valley Authority agreed to lease a medical trailer to the town; local workers added examination and waiting rooms to it. Next, the National Health Service Corps provided money to send Reverend Butziger's wife, Marianne, through a course in practical nursing in Memphis. When the clinic opened on December 1, 1975, she became its full-time staff. By agreement, the Wartburg doctors spend two afternoons per week seeing patients in Deer Lodge.

Meanwhile, the Health Council had been busy on another front. Realizing that a large segment of the people in Morgan County would be unlikely to use any of the three clinics, the Health Council outlined a job description for a family health worker and sought funds to support such a person. After some digging, a sponsor was located in the United Church of Christ. As 1975 opened, the family health worker began her house-to-house rounds contacting, advising and educating those isolated in the outlying sections of the county.

This completes the story of the direct activities of the Health Council. But the interest that it generated was instrumental in the creation of a task force concerned with preventive medicine. Early in 1974 Reverend Butziger arranged with the American Medical Students' Association to host teams who would run eight-week educational campaigns three times a year in the two counties. So far six teams have come and gone, doing such things as training people in dental hygiene and diabetes detection, screening school children for strep throat and vision problems, evaluating home health situations, assisting in the clinics and operating mini-health fairs.

In order to obtain the services of the students, MSP had to promise to provide them with housing, local medical supervision and contacts. It has faithfully performed these duties through the task force. The students live in the homes of volunteers while they work in Morgan and Scott, and each one is assigned a local youth who makes sure that he feels welcome and develops some knowledge of the area. A great deal of good has been accomplished by this program, not only with respect to the people who have benefited from the students' efforts, but also in terms of the familiarity with rural practice that these future doctors and nurses have gained.

The health care picture in the Morgan-Scott area remains bleak. No major work has yet been done in Scott, the poorer and more remote of the two counties. And the three existing clinics in Morgan are not entirely stable. Since they charge only what each patient is able to pay, none of them is self-supporting. Moreover, for it. MSP then recruited volunteers to direct the centers and a regular staff member coordinated the project as a whole. During this second summer the number of volunteers doubled, partially because it became easier to find local young people who were willing to serve as directors and partially because, as MSP became better known outside the area, its ability to attract helpers from faraway places sharply increased. Catholic sisters from Massachusetts, for example, ran the centers at Deer Lodge and Wartburg. The activities in which the youngsters engaged in 1974 roughly mirrored those of 1973, the major difference being the addition of a few work programs. These included bake sales, car washes and coal truck washes to help pay for the field trips. And, with the help of a United Church of Christ youth group from Michigan, local youth and adults painted a house for an elderly woman and renovated the first floor of MSP's farmhouse/office. Altogether, some 323 people served in or were served by the centers.

"Nothing succeeds like success." By the time the 1974 season ended, MSP's initiatives in recreation had gained so much attention that during the winter citizens' committees sprang up in several communities to make plans for 1975. When school let out in June they were ready. Eight towns set up centers and launched ambitious programs which, at mid-summer, were drawing hundreds of youngsters on a regular basis. The list of activities expanded considerably to include newsletter writing, photography, hobo hikes and instruction in self-defense. Summer theater productions were mounted in Petros and Deer Lodge. Several centers also had free lunch programs and rented movies.

Since it was late before a volunteer could be found to coordinate the recreation program in 1976, it contracted in size. Only two towns sponsored centers. But MSP staff were pleased that community residents exercised more active leadership than had been the case in the past. And one significant new project was added to the summer's activities. A group of teenagers from the Philadelphia area spent a week in the homes of local youths, who then reciprocated by becoming the guests of their new friends in Pennsylvania. All parties to this exchange learned from exposure to a culture different from their own.

MSP's staff people are fond of referring to their organization as a catalyst, and no one could wish for a finer illustration of how a catalyst works than this summer project. It began with a valid perception of need. There was no doubt that the young people of the mountain towns were bored and restless from June to September, and that giving them something to do would improve the quality of life in those communities. The Project provided an idea (the recreation program) and a core group of people (the volunteers and staff) willing to work with that idea. Community people were then invited to participate in any way they could. Because community involvement was so assiduously courted and because the need was real and widely recognized, once the program was established it was almost sure to grow. The resources to help the youngsters were already there in Morgan and Scott Counties. What MSP did was to bring these resources together and strike the vital spark.

If recreation has been MSP's clearest success in terms of method, a second task force, the Morgan County Health Council, is outstanding in terms of raw accomplishment. This group's relationship to the Project is somewhat unusual because it was already in existence when MSP was formed in the fall of 1972. Headed by the agricultural extension agent and other public-spirited citizens, the Health Council was working to correct one basic problem, the complete absence of physicians in the county. Almost before MSP set up shop, its people became involved in this effort. Reverend Butziger and a layman, Farrell Kennedy, were appointed to the Health Council's board of directors in September of 1972. When Jim Romer, MSP's first associate director, arrived in Tennessee two months later, he immediately found himself on a council committee. Ever since then, the Health Council and MSP have worked closely together.

For almost 20 years, Morgan County had owned a certain building in the town of Wartburg. The council's original plan was to renovate this property and prevail upon one or more doctors to set up a private clinic there. The renovation was completed, but it soon became clear that no physician was willing to take the financial risk involved in such a venture. The council then began to think in terms of public backing. The National Health Service Corps of the U.S. Department of Health, Education and Welfare would provide the 1973 funding dispute cost the health program its administrator, and as a result the clinics are less tightly managed than they might be. It will be many a day before the people of Morgan-Scott have health facilities even remotely comparable to those in more densely-populated places.

Nevertheless, a beginning has been made. Where before there was a health services' vacuum, people can now get medical and dental attention with tolerable convenience. Some 50 individuals a day are treated at the Wartburg clinic alone, and the number is on the rise. But perhaps more important than the statistics is the consciousness that good care is actually within reach. This awareness, and the confidence that springs from it, offers hope that health conditions will continue to improve.

The senior citizens' task force, like the Health Council, originated independently of MSP. Ten percent of the population of the area is over 65 and the problems of these elderly are aggravated by poverty and isolation. In February of 1973, 25 people got together in Wartburg to establish a senior citizens' council. They obtained a house to use as a center and began a series of weekly meetings. Several Project members were assigned to work with this group. As the year went on, staff people developed a plan to incorporate the council as a non-profit organization and to seek government funding for programs. By March of 1974, the Wartburg group had incorporated as Senior Citizens of Morgan County and two of its members had been appointed to the 16-county East Tennessee Development District Council on Aging. Six months later, Morgan County officials agreed to use $10,000 in revenue-sharing funds to set up an office to provide information and referral services, some limited tranportation to medical facilities, an escort service and social activities for senior citizens.

As time passes, Senior Citizens of Morgan County is becoming an umbrella body for local groups throughout the county. Deer Lodge and Coalfield now have representation in the organization along with Wartburg. The formative stage appears to be over—300 people attended the second annual Senior Citizens Rally—and plans for future action are multiplying. Primary objectives include broadening transportation services for the elderly, founding a nursing home and establishing a multi-purpose center that can be used for meetings, recreational and educational programs, health check-ups, legal consultation, day care and so forth. MSP's involvement with the senior citizens has decreased as their organization has become more solidly established. But one prominent member of the Project council, Rev. Kenneth Phifer, continues to serve as an active consultant, especially in the area of funding.

The fifth MSP task force is the result of a process of steady evolution. From the beginning, all the Project's members have worked in a rather low-key way at community organization. Moreover, the staff has done a good deal of counseling and has cooperated with OEO and welfare workers in helping the needy. The skills, interests and contacts developed through these activities culminated in the formation of the Home Mission Committee in the winter of 1974-1975, when the economic recession led to increased physical suffering in the mountains. Many people were in need of food, fuel and other basic necessities which there was just no money to buy. MSP set up a network of "good neighbors"—they might be employees of the local welfare office or simply concerned individuals—who made it their business to find out when a family was in bad straits. Having identified such a family, the good neighbor drew upon committee resources for immediate aid. He then provided long-range assistance, if necessary, by referral to a social agency. Since the mission committee was established, many thousands of dollars in the form of donated time, clothing, coal, home repairs, health care, transportation and cash have flowed through the system.

Where does the money and material come from? Most of it is donated by church groups and private individuals—the "partners in mission" mentioned earlier. The rest comes from special projects. The Boy Scouts of Deer Lodge, for example, cut and hauled firewood for families unable to provide for themselves. An auction of donated items in the spring of 1975 netted $600. And at Christmas time, people buy clothing for imaginary families of six and donate it to the committee. The clothing is then sold to the poor at greatly reduced prices to serve as gifts. The mission committee is solidly established. Because its program is practical and personal, it appeals to people. It stirs their sympathies and their Christian idealism, offering a simple, direct way of helping one's neighbor.

All the task forces discussed so far have accomplished as much or more than they set out to accomplish. Three others, however, have had to settle for results that did not measure up to expectations. The plans of the first group were imperfectly realized because it could not generate sufficient interest in its work. The other two have been victims of a lack of funds, a lack of administrative leadership and a lack of cooperation from agencies outside MSP.

The Project has always aimed to strengthen pastoral leadership in local churches and to foster a spirit of fellowship and cooperation. In the fall of 1972, it established a task force on church development. This body in turn instituted a series of "church leadership seminars" to which all the area clergy were invited. Initially, the program met with a good response. Between 20 and 30 people came together regularly to hear one of their number discuss the history and tradition of his particular denomination. Once that subject matter was exhausted, however, attendance fell off and in March of 1973 the seminars were dropped.

Activity did not resume for almost a year. In February of 1974, a "spiritual enrichment workshop" was held, the first in a series dealing with communication skills. This series was followed by discussions on the pastoral image, the alcoholic, death and dying, mental health, mental retardation and cultural preconceptions. But then the task force ran out of steam. It is still alive and short courses in areas related to ecumenical action for social justice are offered, but in recent years few church leaders have participated.

The second task force that fell short of its goals came into being toward the end of 1973. At this time, the Project learned that the regional librarian was attempting to develop a books-by-mail program in order to reach people in the more remote sections. Reverend Butziger, who sat on the regional library board, and Jim Romer, who was chairman of the Morgan County board, suggested that the effort be expanded to include the establishment of audio-visual educational centers in Morgan and Scott Counties. The plan was accepted. In early 1974, $20,000 was allocated under the Library Services and Construction Act for four such centers, and MSP was given the responsibility for administering the funds. Staff people visited groups in each of four selected towns to explain the program and ask for community support. This support was quickly forthcoming in the form of physical facilities for the centers. Audio-visual materials of various kinds—films, projectors, tapes and tape recorders—were purchased and by summer the new Community Media Center opened their doors.

But then problems arose. Some centers were better equipped than others, staffing was inadequate and the funding agency would not allow local people to exercise program control. For all these reasons, the media centers were unpopular and their goal of sparking a desire for knowledge among the uneducated has not been achieved. In July of 1974, the Project drew up a proposal for further funding which envisioned upgrading the centers and increasing their services. It was rejected, however, and there the matter stands. The centers are still in operation, but their impact is minimal.

Of all the disappointments that MSP's leadership has suffered over the years, the fate of the task force on economic development is perhaps the most severe. The idea for such a group first surfaced in May 1973. Its purpose was to better the employment outlook in the two counties by founding a community-owned woodcrafts industry. For the first year or so, everything went smoothly. The task force became the Scott-Morgan Community Development Corporation and began laying its plans. It consulted with various experts in the crafts and marketing fields, developed local support for the proposed business, hunted up a building to house it, even picked a name, "The Knot Hole." But the effort on which the members of the group spent most of their time, fund-raising, fell flat. The churches turned them down, foundations and corporations turned them down, a social action agency turned them down twice. Early in 1975, discouraged and frustrated, they postponed further action on the project indefinitely.

The development corporation did not collapse, but it was forced to shift its attention to activities that do not require heavy funding. At present, it is compiling a description in words and pictures of an area the federal government is preparing to turn into a park. This project dovetails to some extent with a broad "environmental impact study" the corporation has undertaken. The information gained from this research, it is hoped, will serve as a basis for sound economic planning in the future.

If three MSP task forces have not lived up to expectations, two have failed entirely. The first of these, the one on day care, has already been mentioned. It was set up in late October 1972, at the third meeting of the Project council. The principal industries in both Morgan and Scott Counties are garment factories that employ mostly women. Clearly, the council felt, the economic and emotional health of local families would be greatly strengthened if low-cost facilities were established where mothers could leave their children during working hours. The task force accepted the job of providing such facilities and went to work with a will. Within eight months arrangements were made to open day care centers in three communities and equipment for them was collected. Most importantly, both the Appalachian Regional Commission and the Tennessee Valley Authority promised financial aid if the task force could secure local matching funds. But there the project came to a halt. Try as it might—and it tried mightily for the next year and a half—the group could not locate any large-scale local funding. The last report of the day care task force appeared in the September 1974 issue of MSP's newsletter, and since then it has faded away.

Shortly after the Project was founded, the council established a task force on education. Except for some research on creating learning opportunities for adults, this group was dormant until the fall of 1973. At that point, however, its members became aware of the Laubach method of literacy training and decided that this approach was well suited to the Morgan-Scott area, where, according to the 1970 census, 18.1% of the population is illiterate. The essence of the Laubach system is expressed in the phrase "each one teach one." Professional instructors teach the first wave of learners, who then teach the second wave, and so on in a self-perpetuating cycle.

The Oneida Methodist Church in Scott County agreed to finance such a program and in February 1974 a consultant from Nashville conducted a workshop to prepare 14 tutors to give literacy training. These 14 took on students with enthusiasm and the project was off to a good start. The task force registered with the National Association for Literacy Advance and formed itself into the Read Better Literacy Association in April. Two months later it began publishing its own newsletter. But then, perhaps because the tutoring proved difficult and the students' progress was slow, the association suddenly lost momentum. It went downhill rapidly, fading in September, dying by the end of the year. Successful only in the sense that it had established a program, the association lived too short a time to have any influence upon reading skills in the Morgan-Scott area.

Since the task force on literacy broke up in late 1974, MSP's career has taken on a new quality. For the first two years of the organization's life, its performance was quite inconsistent. Only about half of the programs it undertook were carried out completely. More recently, however, the Project has settled into a pattern of quiet, steady achievement, making contributions in such diverse fields as mountain crafts, political action, legal aid and education.

It is hard to say exactly when anything that could be called a task force on crafts came into existence. No such group was ever officially mandated by the Project council; it just emerged as an adjunct of MSP's general effort to better the economic opportunities of mountain people. Three craft fair workshops were held at the school in Deer Lodge during the summer and fall of 1974 and people were asked to state what crafts they would like to develop in the future. MSP's involvement at this time was quite informal. By July, however, there was a crafts room at the MSP farmhouse where local workers could display their products. And a year later a general arts and crafts sale was held in Deer Lodge. The task force is composed of the craftsmen themselves and a few MSP people who oversee the delivery of objects for sale to the crafts room and the return flow of money to the workers. At the moment a small enterprise, the crafts business has the potential for growth, as the success of similar efforts in other parts of Appalachia testifies.

A second recent task force has been handled more formally. Late in 1974, a group of six Morgan County citizens, half of whom had close connections with MSP, conceived the idea of filming the political decision-making process at work on the proposed consolidation of county schools. Funding was obtained from the Tennessee Committee for the Humanities; MSP, which furnished an intern to supervise operations, and Roane State Community College became co-sponsors of the project. During the spring of 1975, two students from the college recorded proceedings of the Morgan County Board of Education and the County Court. The film was then edited for continuity, a special effort being made to assure a fair presentation of both sides of the issue.

That summer the film was shown in public meetings in six county towns and citizens were invited to react to it in the presence of their elected representatives. Since the issue was highly emotional, discussion of the viewpoints expressed in the film was often heated, and county officials came away from the meetings with a vivid impression of where their constituents stood. All in all, the project seems to have achieved its purpose, forging a link between the ordinary citizen and local government.

MSP's latest project was launched by a task force calling itself the Equal Justice Team. The group set out to establish a center offering general legal services to those too poor or too far out of the social mainstream to consult commercial firms. By April 1976, $9000 in funding had been obtained through the Commission on Religion in Appalachia (CORA) and applications for other grants were pending. The team hired a paralegal at this time and sent her through a course of training that enabled her to begin seeing clients in mid-July. During the summer it also secured the services of a practicing attorney.

The Equal Justice Team got a home in September when it was named sponsor of the Morgan County Office of Rural Legal Services of Tennessee, a corporation funded by Title XX money. With the resources of this office at its disposal, the task force's original goal of creating a legal aid center has been achieved. As a future direction, it is attempting to establish a network of community volunteers like the one set up by the Home Mission Committee. These volunteers would be given the information and training they need to offer their neighbors reliable welfare benefits counseling.

Despite the importance, both potential and actual, of these three initiatives, the highlight of the Project's last two years has been the establishment of the (Cumberland) Plateau Home School. In mid-1974 a task force was formed to work toward setting up a combination group home and private educational facility. The institution would accept up to 10 resident and 20 day students who exhibited average or above average intelligence but were doing poorly in elementary school. These youngsters would receive individualized training designed to improve their basic skills and foster their emotional development. The ultimate object would be to return the students to the public school system on a level comparable to that of their peers. To help combat the area's 50% school dropout rate, the task force envisioned setting up a network of such institutions throughout the counties if the first one was a success.

At first the project progressed slowly. Public school authorities felt that the Plateau Home School might compete with, rather than supplement, the education they were providing. And, as usual, funding was difficult to find. Consequently, the original plan to open the facility in September 1974 had to be dropped. However, the outlook improved quickly after that. Early in 1975, the United Methodist Church and CORA provided the necessary funds to float the program. As if that were not heartening enough, the superintendent of the Morgan County public system was persuaded to endorse the home school concept. An arrangement was worked out whereby the county would not only refer students to the new institution but would provide financial support for them as well. Greatly encouraged by these developments, the task force accelerated its pace. Three teachers were engaged and plans were finalized for opening the school on October 6, 1975, in public school classrooms in Burrville.

In its first year of operation, the Plateau Home School took in 10 elementary-age children and offered them an intensive curriculum aimed at developing reading and math-science skills. The students monitored their own progress, in cooperation with their parents and a teacher/counselor. So far the results have been striking. Three children have advanced the equivalent of one grade, six have advanced two grades and one especially responsive youngster has jumped three grades! Besides providing academic training, the school sponsored field trips to libraries, zoos and such places as the Museum of Atomic Energy in Oak Ridge to broaden the children's intellectual horizons and further stimulate their desire to learn.

Although the group home aspect of the experiment has not yet materialized, the members of the task force are hopeful that this too can be worked out in the reasonably near future. The school itself seems to be on a firm footing. It was granted state approval early in 1976, making it eligible to receive public educational funds, and has obtained the services of a group of professional consultants who will help review its curriculum as needed and stabilize its operations. Enrollment has doubled; 20 students were on hand when the 1976-1977 school year began on August 30.

When MSP was started in 1972, as we have seen, neither volunteers nor staff had very clear ideas on how a social ministry should be run. For the past four years, they have been learning. They have learned where the money for programs comes from and how to get it, how to organize for action, defuse the opposition and avoid obstacles, how to approach a problem in order to secure local support. It has not been an easy process, but it has resulted in the development of a practical, experienced core group.

A sign of the Project's advancing maturity is that it recently conducted a self-evaluation of some depth, outlining significant problems and suggesting solutions to them. The report concluded in general that the Project was not run tightly enough. It called for a precise statement of purpose to which all of MSP's activities could be clearly related. It recommended that the members focus on one or, at most, a very few projects at any given time. Ties should perhaps be severed with stronger task forces like the Morgan County Health Council. This would free the staff to concentrate on others, like the church development and economic development groups, which were floundering. MSP's structure should be reviewed. The relationship of staff to volunteers, and of council to advisory committee and task forces should be more carefully defined. Decision-making within the council should be formalized. Finally, consideration should be given to clarifying the responsibilities and interrelationships of staff members and to hiring additional staff. The report noted in summary that, although MSP was fundamentally healthy, the recommended changes were necessary to keep it so.

The evaluation report is both timely and useful. There can be little doubt that the Project would benefit from a higher level of formality in its organizational relationships and procedures. For example, "task force" means different things when applied to different groups. The work on church development has been done in the main by staff and council members, not by a semi-independent body. Until fairly recently, in fact, it was called a council program rather than a task force in MSP documents. The senior citizens' group, on the other hand, is only slightly dependent on the Project for help and advice. Other task forces fall somewhere between, so that there is little uniformity in the relationship each group bears to the parent body.

This, in itself, is not a problem. In the course of things, some task forces will naturally develop faster than others and, consequently, the parent organization will be offering a different level of services to one group than it does to another. But MSP has no system for specifying what services a given task force can expect to receive, nor for periodically reexamining and redefining its relationship with each group as that group develops its own resources. This makes it difficult for the leadership to maintain a firm grasp on MSP's priorities, and to apportion valuable staff and volunteer time to reflect these priorities.

Similar clarifications could be made profitably with respect to staff-council and intrastaff relationships. As intimated earlier, the Project is staff-dominated at the highest levels; the council and its executive committee have less real power than the grassroots nature of the organization would seem to demand. Within the staff itself, chains of command and procedures for determining responsibility are largely unspecified. This creates a kind of inner tension as, in the course of their work, staff people pull the Project in several different directions at once.

These problems spring, in part at least, from two causes. First, MSP was founded under the inspiration of highly democratic principles, as would follow from its grassroots orientation. Although this idealism may have been intended to apply only to the decision-making process and not to the implementation of decisions, it has in fact created a general air of individualism in the organization. As a result, the concepts of pattern and consistency receive relatively little emphasis. Second, the Project has historically taken advantage of ministerial opportunities as they arose rather than working from some flexible but definite master plan. The leadership's vision has always been turned outward, not inward, and questions relating to organizational structure have been swept aside in a constant flurry of activity.

One problem not treated in the evaluation report also deserves mention. In theory, the Project works for all the people in Morgan and Scott Counties. In practice, however, most of its activities affect only the northern half of Morgan and the southern half of Scott. Many members feel that the network of contacts and volunteers needs to be expanded to cover the whole area, so that all the people will be taken into account in future planning.

None of these problems is overwhelming, and MSP seems both willing and able to cope with them. What lies ahead for the Project, then? More struggle, no doubt, because its mission is a difficult one. Higher efficiency in conducting its programs, as its growing experience begins to tell. A more complete ecumenism, perhaps; many churches in the area still have no formal association with MSP, and as the organization becomes more established they may take part. And, finally, an ever greater involvement by local people in its work.

Its ecumenism and its skill at attracting grassroots participation must be counted as the Morgan-Scott Project's outstanding qualities. It has been able to lead ordinary people, men and women of different faiths, to work effectively together toward Christian solutions to social problems in which they have a mutual interest. This is certainly no easy task. The group that seeks to serve as a catalyst for both interpersonal and interfaith cooperation must be prepared to deal with conflict. But once the price has been paid, such a group will have made a permanent contribution to the welfare of the area it serves. It will have invested mission in those who will stay when the professionals leave to take other jobs.

8. Building a New Community

*The Center for Community Organization and Area
Development in South Dakota, Minnesota and
Iowa*

How might one go about creating a symbiotic community?
Perhaps by sending out enablers to initiate citizen participation and
promote horizontal communications. This, at least, is the method
employed by the Center for Community Organization and Area
Development (CENCOAD) in the Lower Sioux Basin, a circle of
land covering the southeastern corner of South Dakota, the south-
western corner of Minnesota and the northwestern corner of Iowa.
Since 1969, this area ministry organization has been putting the
people in the cities, towns and open country in touch with one
another and helping them to plan their common future together. No
one with his feet on the ground would say that a perfect community, symbiotic or otherwise, has emerged as a result of CEN-
COAD's efforts. The farmer tending wheat on the open plain still
does not see himself as closely bound to the insurance agent in
Sioux Falls. And the town of Underton is still unhappy with Over-
ton for having succeeded in becoming the county seat in 1884.
Nevertheless, because of CENCOAD, many things have changed
in the Lower Sioux Basin.

A symbiotic community is less arcane than its name suggests.
The term "symbiotic" is derived from nature studies and refers to
the intimate association of two or more dissimilar organisms in a
mutually advantageous relationship. The remora, for example,
clings to the shark, cleaning his gills; in return, it is privileged to
pick up scraps from the hunter's table. Take this concept, apply it
to human society, stretch it a little perhaps, and one forms the

119

notion of a group of different social organisms—towns, cities, farms—that exist side by side and support one another. When the people of an area that is partly urban, partly small-town rural, partly open countryside can live together harmoniously and cooperate for the good of the whole, that is a symbiotic community.

The idea for bringing such a community (also referred to as an "area community") into existence first occurred to Dr. E. W. Mueller in the mid-1960's. He was familiar with the work of Karl Fox at Iowa State University in developing the concept of the functional economic area—an area that was large enough to produce or import enough goods and services to meet the needs of its people. One typical model of a functional economic area was a central city surrounded by its suburbs and, farther out, the rural territory that looked to the city as a major service center. Dr. Mueller was interested in this model because he saw the problems of rural and urban America as closely interrelated. If a rural-urban area was bound together economically in the nature of things, he reasoned, then why could it not also be bound together as a social unit, a community? Could not the resources of the area be so managed that the well-being of all the people was served, the inhabitants of the central city taking an interest in the needs of those in the surrounding territory and vice versa?

It was not long before Dr. Mueller was giving his vision of a new sort of community some publicity. He was quite a visible man in church- and rural-oriented circles. As associate secretary of the Department of Church and Community Planning, Division of Mission Services, Lutheran Council in the U.S.A. and president of the American Country Life Association, he was in a position to present his ideas in talks here and there throughout the country. In the course of time a connection, or series of connections, was made. The result was that in 1969 Augustana College of Sioux Falls, South Dakota, in cooperation with the American Lutheran Church's Board of College Education and National Crisis Board, agreed to fund an agency dedicated to promoting an area community. The agency would be housed by Augustana and would receive support services such as bookkeeping from it. As for the area to be molded into a community, that was not a problem. The Lower Sioux Basin, with its central city of Sioux Falls, its satellite cities of

Brookings, Mitchell and Vermillion, South Dakota and Worthington, Minnesota, its 200-plus small towns and countless farms would do quite well. The 18 counties—four in Iowa, four in Minnesota and 10 in South Dakota—formed the ideal raw material for a symbiotic community.

So, in September 1969, CENCOAD got its start. At first it was a very small operation. Founded as an arm of Augustana, under the direct control of the college's president and board of regents, the Center occupied offices adjacent to the campus. Through the first year of its existence CENCOAD had only two employees, Dr. Mueller and Miss Irma Herrboldt, who served in the dual capacity of secretary and administrative assistant. The immediate need was to make people aware of CENCOAD's presence. Dr. Mueller wrote a number of papers for public consumption that outlined CENCOAD's purpose. He also did a lot of public speaking, explaining the agency to any groups interested enough to listen. In the time he could spare from this schedule of educational work, he also launched his active campaign to foster community in the Basin. His strategy had been planned out in advance and within a few months he was beginning to put it into practice.

As far as its place in the world of area ministry organizations is concerned, CENCOAD is an action group with no support or advisory functions. It is a rather unusual sort of action group, though. CENCOAD does not run programs that do things for people, in the usual sense. For example, one would not find the organization involved in administering a meals program for the elderly or a summer recreation program for youth. Rather, CENCOAD runs programs that help people do things for themselves. The organization gives them a vision of cooperative action and equips them with the necessary understanding and skills to make this vision real. The meals and the recreation are available in CENCOAD's service area, but local people, and not a professional agency, have done the principal work in bringing them about.

This emphasis on self-help does not spring from a particularly conservative bias, but from the profound conviction that much good can be done from a Christian point of view through citizen participation in the American political system. Dr. Mueller and his associates consider the central purpose of that system to be the delivery of services in response to people's needs. CENCOAD is in the business of seeing to it that people know how to express their needs and how to influence the system to fulfill them. It is social ministry—orienting the temporal order to Christ, in the language of Vatican II—with a democratic twist. Instead of focusing on the institutional Church as bearer of the ministry, CENCOAD focuses on ordinary Christian people working in their communities through the existing secular power structure.

The primary impediment to this ministerial approach is, of course, that ordinary people are usually not in close touch with the power structure. The development of the United States has been characterized by a shift in political and economic power away from the town and county to the state and federal levels. As a result, the average citizen has tended to lose faith in his ability to effect change through the democratic process. Government is no longer accessible. He often finds himself looking at it as through a telescope; it is massive, it is monolithic, it is remote and, most importantly, it is indifferent to his small concerns. No wonder, then, that many Americans rarely participate in the political system except to vote and that, for them, government is not a living source of useful services but a dull and rather pompous show played out on a TV screen.

CENCOAD hopes to strengthen the link between the average citizen and government on all levels. It encourages him to work with local government where that is appropriate and to address himself to state and federal agencies on problems of greater scope. CENCOAD also tries to combat the people's sense of powerlessness by making them aware that although each person may reside in a small community that lacks political "clout," at the same time he is part of a much larger community with great potential. If he wishes to act, he may find allies in this area community who will join in the effort. He is not alone.

Because it helps citizens organize for political action, the agency sometimes antagonizes town and county officials who feel that their bailiwick is being invaded. But this sort of tension has become relatively rare as CENCOAD has won acceptance in the territory, and it never was the result of aggression on the organization's part. CENCOAD does not see itself as being anti-establishment in any way. Its object is to supplement the work of local authorities and to stimulate them to greater activity by supplying a model for citizen participation in decision-making.

CENCOAD comes to its task armed with the viewpoints and to some extent the resources of higher education and the Church. The involvement of higher education comes, of course, through Augustana's sponsorship of the agency. The college feels a responsibility to apply the insights of the academic community to the problems of the community at large. Helping to launch and sustain such an organization as CENCOAD is one way of being of service to its home area. The involvement of the Church—or, rather Churches, for CENCOAD is ecumenical both in theory and practice—is even more immediate. The bulk of the organization's initial funding came from the American Lutheran Church. All its staff people but two are clergy or religious. A substantial part of its services are directed at the congregations of the Sioux Falls area. And all its work, even that which seems at first glance to be entirely secular, is done in conscious obedience to the Christian commandment to love your neighbor. Again, CENCOAD's goal is not just to make democracy work, but to make democracy work for the building up of the Kingdom of God.

CENCOAD's present motto is "People Inventing the Future Together." It emphasizes progress through community action, saying, in effect, "We in the Lower Sioux Basin are all in this together." This concept builds upon and incorporates a notion expressed in the organization's original motto, "The Unit and the Unity," which projected a definite sort of community. Basing himself on the concept of symbiosis, Dr. Mueller aimed at developing an area community created by a combination of self-interest and common interest. Individual units—groups, towns, counties, alliances of counties—were urged to do independently whatever they could do with excellence, focusing on their own needs. So, for example, one town opened a youth center, the people of several school districts participated in a process designed to clarify their attitudes toward education, and an agency serving the elderly of six counties was established. At the same time, however, constant attention was to be paid to the unity, the area as a whole. Units were encouraged to work together whenever necessary and the welfare of the entire Lower Sioux Basin was to be taken into account in formulating and implementing plans.

The phrase, "The Unit and the Unity," then, looked toward the day when the rugged, self-reliant people of the South Dakota prairies, while continuing to indulge that tendency toward independent action that was so deeply imbedded in their culture, would learn to see themselves as part of a larger community than they were used to envisioning. This area community already existed after a fashion. It existed as a functional economic area, as we have noted. And the greater part of it existed on paper as a substate planning and development district, duly constituted by the state of South Dakota and represented by the Southeastern Council of Governments. CENCOAD's problem was to make it emerge more solidly by raising the consciousness of the people and by getting them to accept cooperative planning as a way of life. It was this monumental task that Dr. Mueller and his single assistant tackled in the fall of 1969.

The strategy CENCOAD employed, once the preliminary educational work was well under way, centers around the key word "catalyst." If the organization was to concentrate on helping people help themselves, what could its role be? Dr. Mueller was well aware that the great obstacles to effective citizen participation in the workings of the political system were the ignorance and apathy we have already noted. People could usually identify their needs if they sat down and thought about things for a moment. But once those needs were identified, they had no idea how to proceed in meeting them, and tended just to dismiss the matter with a shrug and a stoical "Well, that's the way it is." They took a negative, almost mystical view of their position vis-a-vis government instead of a positive, practical one. In reality, all that was needed was to bring their chosen objectives to the attention of the right officials, be able to apply a certain amount of pressure and be in a position to actually use whatever help was forthcoming. It was, in simplest terms, a matter of knowing the ropes.

Dr. Mueller's idea was to provide an agency, CENCOAD, that could offer both knowledge and motivation to the people. Once needs surfaced, CENCOAD would be available to groups of citizens at no cost to help them work and plan together, identify and contact those officials in their communities and elsewhere who made the essential decisions, identify sources of financial backing and draw up applications to obtain it. Through the expertise of its staff in these and other areas, CENCOAD would act as a catalyst to the process by which people worked out their problems in concert.

CENCOAD's mode of operating evolved very quickly in 1970. The first step was to hire more staff; Delano Lind, a Lutheran pastor with experience in community development, became CENCOAD's third employee. Through most of the year, the organization worked rather like a training and consulting office. Among other tasks, Reverend Lind conducted training sessions for local pastors and for citizens' groups that came to the Center with a problem. He also ran multitown and multicounty workshops aimed at improving communications among units within the area. In the consulting line, CENCOAD got involved in a conference on aging. It convened a planning committee for the conference, contributed staff time and secretarial services, recruited and trained people to head discussion groups and waged a campaign to secure attendance. Finally, CENCOAD supplied some outside organizations directly with support services. The most prominent recipients of these services were MIKOTA Opportunities, Inc., a multicounty economic development agency, and the MID Areawide Health Planning Council.

Training and consulting were valuable activities, but they provided limited coverage. The Lower Sioux Basin includes some 11,000 square miles and, with a small staff, CENCOAD could not hope to help all or even most of the groups and individuals needing help. Late in 1970, a decision was made to broaden the organization's range, and Reverend Lind was given the responsibility for inventing a practical way to achieve this goal. He had a "starter" idea on which to base his thinking. For some time, Dr. Mueller had been experimenting with the notion of employing local people as part-time workers to promote community development among their own neighbors. Reverend Lind adopted this approach and drew from it a full-blown program. While Dr. Mueller had projected calling his local workers "consultants," Reverend Lind renamed them "enablers," because they enabled something to be done. He invented a technique for identifying people with the natural qualifications to serve as enablers. He designed a training program for them. Finally, he appointed himself an "enabler to enablers," someone the new workers could come to for help and advice when they got bogged down in the performance of their unfamiliar duties.

This program was destined to serve as the basis for most of the community development work CENCOAD would do. Enablers were first used in connection with a project entitled "Training Low Income Residents to Increase Their Knowledge of Their Social Situations," that was launched in March 1971. It was approved for support under Title I of the Higher Education Act, matching funds being provided by Augustana College.

As the project's title implies, it focused on education rather than action. The object was to give the residents of a poor section of Sioux Falls some perspective on the problems prevalent in their area and to acquaint them with the structures through which these problems might be addressed. Eight low-income people from the community were hired to move about in the different neighborhoods to observe, to listen to complaints and to help their peers understand the socio-economic situation in which they found themselves. They were trained for their task by consultants whom Reverend Lind had gathered from a number of different organizations: the Sioux Falls Continuing Education Center (a cooperative institution in which Augustana College, Sioux Falls College and the North American Baptist Seminary participate), the United Way Community Planning Council of Sioux Falls and the Problems in Living Center.

An evaluation conducted in 1972 concluded that the project had shown how institutions of higher learning could work with the poor to their mutual benefit. It had also established that the most productive way to help any community was to operate through indigenous people rather than through "outside experts." Yet the practical results were undramatic. The welfare rolls did not decrease; the residents' ability to cope with their problems did not improve sharply.

The value of this particular experiment was perhaps greater to CENCOAD itself than to the people it was designed to help, because it led the organization to develop a new model for the use of enablers that has since served it very well. But more of that in a moment. Even though CENCOAD's experience with the Sioux Falls project was somewhat frustrating, 1971 was still a year of considerable accomplishment. A paper on CENCOAD services published in November lists 24 separate areas of involvement, some more highly developed than others, but all testifying to the agency's growing impact. Besides continuing the activities begun earlier (speaking engagements, training sessions, workshops), CENCOAD sponsored or helped organize conferences on housing, recreation, education and welfare; helped set up senior citizens' centers in several towns; involved students in study projects related to the symbiotic community; helped farmers whose crops had been damaged to seek aid from the Farmers' Home Administration and the Small Business Administration; provided support and office services to the Welfare Rights Organization, the State Low Income Council and the Minnehaha Indian Club; and worked to help educate people in ecology and pollution control. All of these efforts bore fruit in one way or another and helped establish CENCOAD as one of the leading public-interest agencies in the Lower Sioux Basin.

In 1972, CENCOAD concentrated on two priorities. The first involved stabilizing the agency's reputation, which was accomplished by continuing and in some cases expanding the services initiated in 1971 or earlier, especially workshops. The second priority was to move in new directions, mount new programs. This growth was made possible in part by the support CENCOAD received from the Franciscan Sisters of Rochester, Minnesota, who made available two members of their community, Sisters Mary Eliot Crowley and Marlys Ann Jax, as full-time staff persons.

Community workshops had always been prominent among the services CENCOAD offered, and the period 1972-73 marked the high point of its activities along these lines. In 1972, the agency received a grant under the Higher Education Act for a part-time staff person to specialize in organizing workshops, and this employee set up 12 of them serving groups in Sioux Falls and in eight surrounding communities. Six of these workshops dealt with senior citizens and the problems related to retirement generally. Of the remaining six, three were concerned with community services, one focused on improving the business climate in a small town, one aimed at giving visibility to CENCOAD's efforts at community development and one exposed the needs of and identified the services available to local handicapped persons. Altogether, 1404 people participated in the workshops and in the planning sessions that preceded them; the cost of the project was $5400.

What happens at a CENCOAD workshop? Perhaps the matter can best be explained by an example. Early in 1972, a Lutheran minister in a small town outside Sioux Falls contacted the agency about a long-standing conflict which was tearing the fabric of his community. The storm centered around the school board, which had apparently purchased some land without clearly explaining the reason to its constituency. Dr. Mueller suggested that the pastor determine if the citizens wanted CENCOAD to help them resolve this conflict. They did. A group of some 30 couples was formed and on April 6, Dr. Mueller made a presentation before these men and women in which he discussed community development, stressing the importance of effective communication in preventing misunderstandings and wounded feelings.

Next he divided the assemblage into small groups and asked them to clarify the issues involved in the conflict and suggest a course of action. When the evening was over, the citizens elected a committee to carry the issues which had been surfaced to the entire community. They were to get a reaction from the community and take whatever steps were necessary to resolve the conflict in the light of this reaction. In accord with its philosophy, CENCOAD's involvement in the whole process of community reconciliation was simply to set that process in motion. Armed with a new committee and the small group method of communication and analysis, the people themselves were prepared to carry on from there.

The two new programs which dominated the year 1972 are both connected with major thrusts in CENCOAD's overall career. As we have seen, senior citizens had absorbed a good share of the organization's attention almost from the beginning. The most significant result of the 1970 conference on aging that CENCOAD had helped organize was the creation of the six-county Areawide Project on Aging in late 1971. The Project was designed to be spun off as an independent agency when it had gained enough strength, and throughout 1972 the CENCOAD staff worked to bring it to maturity. CENCOAD provided seed money for its new brain child, did the groundwork to get it functioning, obtained grants to sustain it. Finally, in October, CENCOAD set it free, although a consultative relationship was maintained and CENCOAD continued to provide training for the Project's staff and workers. The Areawide Project has since established no less than 21 senior citizens' centers throughout the Basin and is presently developing a service package for them.

The second program is of pivotal importance in CENCOAD's career; much of the organization's later effectiveness stems from the ideas and techniques worked out in connection with it. The results of the 1971 project which had employed enablers to educate low-income residents of Sioux Falls had convinced the CEN-COAD staff that it had taken the wrong approach to neighborhood development. When staff members began to think about launching community development efforts in the rural parts of the area, then, they looked for a new model. Over a period of months in 1972, they designed a revised version of the enabler program. For the third time, funds were applied for under Title I of the Higher Education Act, for the third time they were granted, and by the middle of the year newly trained enablers were sprinkled among the small towns and hamlets of the Basin.

Like the men and women employed in the Sioux Falls project, these enablers were local people who worked part-time (eight hours per week) in their own communities. They were not professional social workers in any sense. They were farmers, teachers, housewives, clergymen, retirees, businessmen, involved citizens in every walk of life. All that was required of candidates was that they be mature, have an interest in the local community, be able to relate well with others and be sensitive to problems associated with race, poverty and social pluralism. Unlike the Sioux Falls enablers, however, they were oriented toward action more than education. Instead of merely equipping people with knowledge of their social situation, these community workers equipped them with the means of influencing it.

Since 1972, the enablers have been CENCOAD's front-line

troops in the battle to help citizens bring growth to the Lower Sioux Basin. This is not to say that staff members do not have considerable contact with the people. But staff activities tend to be educational or supportive in nature: giving talks, conducting workshops, doing research or working on a grant proposal. Enablers are trained in the areas of understanding community, personal and group relations, leadership, organizational development, community organization, planning and training of others. They do the bulk of the actual work of helping people surface their concerns, get organized and develop programs to act. Earlier, we identified CENCOAD as a catalyst. The enablers are the point at which catalyst and elements meet, producing change.

CENCOAD has employed some 115 enablers over the years. At one time in 1972 or 1973 the organization had over 30; in 1974, when funds were scarce, it had only a handful. As we shall see, enablers get involved in all kinds of different projects. Yet there is some uniformity in their work, as there is uniformity in the approach to community problems that CENCOAD trains them to take. Once a man or woman (more likely the latter; about two-thirds of CENCOAD's field workers have been women) has been prepared to act as an enabler, he or she returns home to listen, observe and tune in on community needs. The enabler identifies and supports existing action organizations through which community development programs might be channeled. Should a process be set in motion to resolve a problem, he coordinates the activities of local groups and serves as a contact between these groups and outside human or material resources. He helps gather data, set goals and strategies, plan, analyze and evaluate. Finally, the enabler assumes that role which is absolutely indispensable for the success of any volunteer organization: he becomes the doer of chores, the runner of errands. He makes phone calls, plans meetings and makes sure they are actually held, sets up the chairs in the meeting hall, sees to it that everybody is informed about everything, keeps tabs on progress, makes surveys, soothes ruffled feelings. If level of involvement is the measure, the enabler more often than not is the center of the community task group.

And yet he is not its official head. Again, a CENCOAD enabler is one who enables others to do things. His work lies in the background; he functions sometimes as a secretary, but never as a president. The teenagers in the town of Parker, for example, wanted a youth center, but did not know how to go about getting one. The enabler stepped in and started a county youth group. This failed. She then organized a town group by working through the school. From this point on she was able to operate behind the scenes, supporting the young people and making connections for them. Before very long, $2000 was raised and the youth center became a reality. On another occasion, the people of Canton needed a hospital. The CENCOAD enabler, who was knowledgeable about grants, persuaded the citizens' group which was sponsoring the hospital to hire a professional fund raiser, with whom he then collaborated. The project began in June 1972 and terminated with the opening of the new hospital in October 1975, after the citizens' group had raised over one and a half million dollars.

The 1972 Title I grant, with matching funds from Augustana College, totaled $45,600. It paid the salaries of 16 enablers, and these men and women worked on 71 projects that year and the next. Meanwhile, the Campaign for Human Development had also funded enabler positions, so CENCOAD was able to be present in a great many places throughout its service area. Besides the youth center in Parker and the hospital in Canton, CENCOAD people in 1972-1973 assisted groups in putting together a directory of civic organizations in Sioux Falls; setting up a Homemaker service in Turner County; organizing community dialogues on various issues; starting senior citizen centers in several towns; organizing farmers in Moody and Minnehaha counties to work with the Farmers' Home Administration to get a rural water system installed; setting up economic development workshops in McCook County; establishing day care centers here and there; starting a Retired Senior Volunteer Program in Canton; building eight apartments for low-income elderly people in Humboldt; organizing efforts of business people to see what might be done about the railroad's plan to abandon lines in Union, Turner, Lincoln and McCook counties; and getting bicycles registered in Vermillion, to name just a few. The Title I grant alone "enabled" projects in which almost 9000 people participated and which generated 1.8 million dollars in revenue for various worthy causes.

Generally speaking, 1973 was as good a year as 1972 had been. In some ways it was better. The enablers became more effective as they gained experience; the staff expanded once more just before the beginning of the year, allowing for the establishment of a new program aimed at the clergy of the area; a newsletter, appropriately called *People!*, was begun; and the organization as a whole hummed with activity. By 1973, there was a strong feeling that Dr. Mueller's dream of an area community was beginning to have a substantial impact.

In spite of CENCOAD's overall progress, however, two of its projects died uneasy deaths in 1973, one because it was premature and the other as a result of bureaucratic entanglements. MIKOTA Opportunities, Inc., the economic development agency whose name is an anagram of Minnesota-Iowa-Dakota, had been formed by a group of area businessmen before CENCOAD was started. It obtained some funds from the state government at Pierre for waging a campaign to attract industry into the area and set about the task of spreading the gospel of economic development. But the different towns, clinging to their individualistic traditions, saw MIKOTA's efforts at area development as a threat to their own developmental schemes and would not support it. From 1970 on CENCOAD did all it could to bolster the organization, donating staff and secretarial time and helping to promote its ideas. Staff people even developed and published rather elaborate economic/political profiles of Clay and Turner Counties to serve as a basis for cooperative planning. But it did not work in the long run; attitudes could not be changed so quickly. MIKOTA remained active for about five years, gathering data and encouraging the development of economic potential wherever possible. Then it went dormant, and has remained dormant ever since.

The MID Areawide Health Planning Council was formed with CENCOAD's help in 1970 to do just what its name states: draw up a comprehensive health care plan for a nine-county area covering parts of Minnesota, Iowa and South Dakota. It was a citizens' group like MIKOTA, made up of 49% health care providers and 51% health care consumers. CENCOAD helped the members to conduct a survey of health needs and resources and to write up a proposal for a federal grant. At this point, unfortunately, complications arose. The health council had hoped that all the counties involved could share in the grant on an equal basis. But the money had to be channeled through the Southeastern Council of Governments. The leadership of this organization opted to retain control of all funds, requiring the out-of-state counties to buy in via contracts. This plan proved unacceptable to county authorities in Iowa and Minnesota, so the grant request was not pursued further and the health council was never established.

The new staff member who had joined CENCOAD in the latter part of 1972 was Rev. Lawrence Murtagh, a trained supervisor in Clinical Pastoral Education (CPE). His coming added a new dimension to the organization's work. Father Murtagh had developed an adaptation of the standard CPE program, one that was specifically aimed at pastors of rural parishes. Its purpose was to educate these clergymen to relate the gospel to the socio-economic aspects of community life through their preaching and pastoral visitation. There was to be nothing abstract about the application of the gospel message. Rather, the priests and ministers in the program were to direct sermons and conversations toward current issues that parishioners were actually facing in their daily lives.

Father Murtagh spent a great deal of time in 1973 traveling throughout the area, getting acquainted with the clergy of all the denominations and giving a talk wherever he could find a small audience. He also held a number of workshops and conducted a series of "mini-CPE units" in which a total of 89 pastors participated, meeting one day a week for six weeks. In the fall, the model he had designed was accredited by the national CPE organization. Since that time Father has done his teaching primarily through 30-week courses which cover such topics as "Land Use," "Rural Health Systems," "Who Will Control American Agriculture?" and "Life Styles in Rural America."

The adapted CPE program not only familiarizes pastors with social systems and social issues in their communities but prepares them to assume an active part in community affairs as well. This "active part" may take either or both of two forms. First, the pastor may lend a hand himself, working for the United Fund in his town, helping out in the youth center, serving on the school board, and so forth. More importantly for the town as a whole, he may encourage his congregation to become involved with the community, thus multiplying his impact.

In Father Murtagh's view, this task of consciously inserting the gospel message into the flow of community life is by nature an ecumenical one. He is fond of quoting Dr. Mueller's dictum to the effect that there are no Catholic or Lutheran or Methodist soil conservation districts. The community's social, political and economic problems are everyone's problems, and the denominations have a duty to cooperate in bringing the Christian perspective to bear upon them. He is a Catholic priest. His program was funded by Lutheran Brotherhood before it was absorbed into the general CENCOAD budget. And he has taught, to date, clergy of nine denominations, usually in mixed groups. As is typical of CENCOAD projects, the CPE program seeks to serve the entire area by taking a very broad approach to its work.

While Father Murtagh was developing CPE, the staff and enablers of CENCOAD were busy on many fronts. Working through existing institutions as usual, an enabler persuaded the city council of Canistota to donate an unused building for a senior citizens' center and provide materials with which to remodel it. Another helped the citizens of a small town influence the outcome of a referendum on purchasing some abandoned railroad land. Perhaps the most interesting, if not the most spectacular, self-help project in which CENCOAD was involved in 1973 was CRUD— Community Recyclers of Usable Discards. Two Augustana students were the prime movers behind CRUD, a non-profit organization for collecting, storing and selling recyclable trash. In spite of problems with volunteers (after a couple of tours of duty at the collection points, people tended to lose interest), and with the help of the National Guard, CRUD has survived and is still active in Sioux Falls.

Over the years, CENCOAD had received a number of requests to help iron out community problems related to the local school. It had become increasingly clear to the organization's staff that the public education system was a leading occasion of discord in the small towns that dotted the area. Often parents misunderstood or simply opposed the content of courses their children were offered. Often there was disagreement over spending for educational purposes. Very often, school-related conflict was the residue of a consolidation which may have taken place ten years earlier. There was an obvious need for some sort of program which would allow people to work out their differences amicably, and early in 1973 CENCOAD resolved to provide such a program.

The result of the organization's efforts was a plan and a grant. The grant for $11,700 came from the South Dakota Committee on the Humanities in September. The plan was to provide a sort of workshop for communities torn or threatened by school-related conflicts. In this workshop, interested citizens and a professor in one of the humanities at a local college would meet and try to clarify the dimensions of the conflict. CENCOAD hoped to identify the values which determined the direction local education was taking and the often opposed values implicit in citizen reaction to this direction. Discussion would lead to the creation of some structure such as a conference or task group which could resolve the conflict and develop an action plan having broad support in the community. In the nine months the program was in force, eight school districts were helped. No revolutionary changes resulted. But people came to understand more of the whys and wherefores of their local schools and are in a better position to make a contribution to them in the future.

The school program extended through June of 1974, by which time CENCOAD had entered a brief period of relative inactivity. The slowdown was not caused by a loss of will on the organization's part nor by the failure of any key projects. It was due, very simply, to a lack of money. As noted, CENCOAD was originally funded in 1969 by grants from Augustana College and two agencies of the American Lutheran Church. These grants all carried a time limit of three years, so by the end of 1972 CENCOAD was in a precarious financial position. Augustana kept the organization afloat with supplemental funds for salaries and office expenses, but there was precious little money left over for programs. If CEN-COAD wanted to provide some major service that the staff alone could not deliver, a grant had to be obtained to pay for it. In 1972 and 1973, as we have seen, the organization succeeded in getting such grants. An application for funds to hire enablers for 1974 was turned down, however, and CENCOAD's corps of community workers, and thus the volume of work it could generate, declined drastically.

A few months later, Augustana College began to feel the pinch applied by a depressed national economy, and a decision was made to cease underwriting CENCOAD's operating budget. This action provoked a very serious crisis. Fortunately, however, CENCOAD had taken steps to prepare itself for such a turn of events. From the very beginning, Dr. Mueller had recognized his relative lack of skill in fund-raising and business administration. He was aware, of course, that these skills were needed within the organization if it were to survive when the original funding ran out. Partly for these reasons, he had in 1970 designed a unique one-year internship for Victor Pavlenko, a Lutheran seminary student who through training, practical experience and family background was familiar with business procedures. After graduating from the seminary, Reverend Pavlenko kept up his ties with CENCOAD serving, for example, as the enabler who helped the people of Canton raise 1.5 million dollars to build a hospital. When it began to appear in the summer of 1973 that severe financial problems were imminent, he was offered a full-time position on the staff.

At the time of the crisis in 1974, then, Reverend Pavlenko was on hand to act as spokesman for CENCOAD on money matters. He went to Augustana's board of regents with a series of alternatives for the future, one of which was to close down permanently. The board, well aware of the contribution CENCOAD was making to the area, rejected this possibility and set up a system whereby the organization could borrow from Augustana in order to remain in operation. It also approved a restructuring of CENCOAD which Reverend Pavlenko had suggested with a view to making it financially independent in the long run.

This restructuring consisted in transforming the organization into a non-profit corporation, which would entitle it to seek financial support from the public at large. A 15-member inter-denominational board of directors was assembled in July 1974 to head the new corporation, and CENCOAD, Inc. officially registered with the state of South Dakota on January 8, 1975. Since then, the organization has been attempting to reach the point where as much of its budget as possible is drawn from local contributions, thus cementing its identification with the area which it has served for seven years. Partially because CENCOAD's general visibility is poor, however, the achievement of this goal is still far away.

It may seem strange that CENCOAD's financial problem would be complicated by low visibility. After all, it works primarily through direct contact with local people and has obviously done a great deal of good. This is true, but it is also true that CENCOAD is basically an office affiliated with a college. It is not a people's group in any easily recognizable way. In addition, even though Dr. Mueller spent a great deal of time in the early years spreading CENCOAD's message through the Lower Sioux Basin, he chose a very quiet and self-effacing operating style for the organization. Very often the people of a given town do not even know that Mary Jones who did all the work on the community project is a CENCOAD enabler. The workers in the field have been trained, in line with CENCOAD's general philosophy, to emphasize citizen initiative and this has meant deemphasizing the importance of their own roles.

In spite of this orientation, it was clearly necessary to make CENCOAD better known if it were to mount an effective appeal for public support. The board of directors accordingly decided in 1974 to render CENCOAD audible, if not visible, by authorizing a series of radio "spots" which explained the organization's purpose and activities. Up to the present, 98 three- to five-minute programs have been produced and aired. The newsletter *People!*, which did not reach a sufficiently broad audience, was dropped and its budget appropriated for this new campaign. In addition, a Franciscan sister on the CENCOAD staff was assigned to handle media relations and oversee publicity. One of her most recent projects has been cooperating with the University of Minnesota in the creation of three ten-minute films dealing with current CENCOAD activities. In general, an ongoing effort was launched to give CENCOAD a firm, positive image that will attract the steady backing it needs to survive over the long haul.

In spite of the difficulties it had to face, CENCOAD did manage to start an important new program in the spring of 1974. As Father Murtagh's CPE work progressed, he and Dr. Mueller discovered that although the various churches cared for themselves and their members, they did not place much emphasis on caring for their communities as such. CPE was designed to better this situation through its focus on involving the pastor and congregation in the life of the community. But the staff felt that a more intensive training device was needed to impress upon clergy and interested laity that they had a responsibility to work for the common welfare. From this line of thinking came a new creation, the Caring for Community Institutes.

The institutes are three-day or seven-day "experiences" held several times a year, in which some 20 participants live, work, celebrate liturgies, eat and play together while exploring such basic questions as the relation of the gospel to the human situation and the role of church in the community at large. Instruction is provided by CENCOAD staff in a series of formal lectures. In the November 1974 institute, for instance, they spoke on "Praising, Working, Living," "Preacher and Preaching," "Beyond the Stable Flock," "Horizons Unlimited (Parish and Community)," "Our Turf," "Reaching In and Reaching Out," "The Big Sky (A Global View)" and "To Build the City of Man." The material presented in these lectures becomes the subject of small group discussions where the participants express their own views on what the staff has offered and get the reactions of their peers. Finally, each man and woman is placed in a "primary group" designed to generate an atmosphere of trust and cooperation and to develop interpersonal skills. The approach is theological and Scriptural, aiming ultimately at placing the idea of caring for community in the context of the broad mission of the Church.

The Institutes, the CPE program, and the consultative services CENCOAD offers to local churches in fields like program development and leadership training represent an intensification of its campaign to bring the sphere of the sacred more intimately into contact with the sphere of the secular. This has always been one of the principles underlying CENCOAD's activities. But in 1973 and 1974, its interest in the role of the established Church in actual community development increased greatly. This thrust is now firmly established, and it will presumably continue to play a prominent part in the organization's efforts to "build the city of man" in its chosen territory.

One of the reasons CENCOAD's work with congregations has expanded is the steady growth of its staff. A third Franciscan sister and a former student at Augustana have joined in the past three years, bringing the number of full-time people to eight. CENCOAD now has the flexibility to cover many fronts at once or to focus very heavily on one front for a time just by a simple shift of personnel. The Caring for Community Institutes, for example, can offer a very intensive, personalized sort of learning because as many as eight staffers can and sometimes do participate as lecturers and group leaders. And when there is no need for such concentration, the workers can disperse to various posts, helping the enablers, running workshops, becoming acquainted with local clergy, preparing media releases and so on. It is a far cry from the days when Dr. Mueller and his secretary handled everything themselves.

There has also been a change in leadership. Dr. Mueller, who refers to himself rather jauntily as a senior citizen, retired to become director emeritus on January 1, 1975. A man of wisdom, dedication and broad experience, he founded the innovative organization, nursed it along in the first years, saw it through crises, gathered a skilled and dedicated staff for it, and guided it to its initial accomplishments. When Dr. Mueller relinquished the directorship he could do so with the satisfaction of knowing that he had taken a new idea and made it work.

Reverend Pavlenko became the new director. He took over the reins at quite a propitious time. The U.S. Office of Education had just allotted $150,000 to CENCOAD to provide educational services to citizens interested in the issue of land use. Hard decisions on such questions as soil erosion, soil sedimentation, rural and urban development, and conservation would have to be made in the near future. CENCOAD wanted to help local people prepare themselves to face these important choices in an intelligent and informed way. Moreover, if the Basin were ever to become a real community, its citizens had to be able to join together in discussing what to do with their basic resource—the land.

The first phase of the land use project was completed early in 1976 and evaluated a few months later. According to the evaluation report, county forums, media announcements and the efforts of the enablers had increased people's awareness of land use problems and the need for future planning. It concluded, however, that much still needed to be done before the ultimate goal of the project, the formation of public policy favorable to responsible land use, could be considered achieved. How well CENCOAD is able to carry through a program of this magnitude, requiring the cooperation of a large number of individuals and organizations throughout the area, remains to be seen.

Although the focus of the land use project is educational, some of CENCOAD's enablers have taken the next logical step and encouraged action on related issues within their own communities. One, for example, helped locate a suitable site for a sanitary landfill. And, of course, community development efforts in fields other than land use are constantly being pursued in line with CENCOAD's general philosophy. In an attempt to offer action-oriented enablers more concrete guidance than their training sessions provide, CENCOAD staff members have recently produced a series of handbooks that describe the dynamics of community development and suggest a step-by-step process which an organizer might follow. The principal text in this series, which is entitled *Involving Citizens in Community,* gives an overview of the task at hand, moving from a discussion of "the talking stage" through "goal setting" and "finding resources" to "celebration and evaluation." More specific publications cover team-building, improving communication skills, organizing and conducting meetings and goal setting.

The land use program has benefited from activity in another area as well. Since 1972, CENCOAD has been investing time and money in the development of a computerized data bank on certain topics of interest to the organization. Paul Reeg, a CENCOAD enabler, was assigned in 1974 to work full time toward this goal. First, a file was completed in 12,000 persons in the Basin. Then the staff began assembling information on every organization in the area, including businesses and units of local government. Both individuals and organizations were catalogued according to their area of concern (the environment, economic development, services to senior citizens, and so on) and the geographical territory they cover. The data bank also contains information on the major difficulties the organizations have overcome. In this way, people faced with a particular problem can easily be put in contact with those who have already dealt with that problem. Such a system is obviously of great value for areawide land use planning, and it has played a significant part in CENCOAD's efforts in that direction.

The data bank provides information useful in a wide variety of situations. CENCOAD's staff also wanted the capability to determine how citizens felt about specific issues. Consequently, in 1975, the organization obtained the right to use a system developed by the Forum Foundation of Seattle. An opinionnaire which probes values and attitudes on various questions is administered to a random sample of people in the target group—in this case, the population of the Lower Sioux Basin. The responses to these opinionnaires are then computerized, so that anyone who wants to know the public's disposition on a certain question can get an answer, or at least a strong indication, simply by pressing a button. This survey device, which elicited opinions from 3800 citizens during the first phase of the land use program alone, has many uses. It can help CENCOAD choose and prioritize its goals. It can lessen the chance of making public relations errors. If careful records are kept of results over a span of time, the system can indicate to what extent a community spirit is growing in the Basin. Perhaps most importantly, when the opinionnaires are designed in cooperation with public officials, they put CENCOAD in the position of being able to advise those in power with respect to specific decisions. The survey becomes, then, another tool for ensuring citizen participation in the political process.

The other activities which currently occupy CENCOAD staff are largely routine. The workshops, the training sessions, the Caring for Community Institutes, the speaking engagements, the work with outside organizations all continue. A joint project with South Dakota State University has just been completed. It involved helping arrange county-level meetings for people concerned about community-based health care. Also on July 1, 1976, CENCOAD launched a three-year citizen education project on water supply management, funded for $82,000 by the U.S. Office of Education and the Northwest Area Foundation. A contract to provide leadership training for officers of South Dakota's senior citizens' centers through 1977 was recently signed. Finally, the organization has tested a method of establishing communication hookups with people in other parts of the United States and in foreign countries. A satellite was used for this experiment, and CENCOAD is presently awaiting the results of an application to NASA for more satellite time. If this request is granted, the staff will set up international telephone conferences on various topics of interest to the citizens of its service area.

CENCOAD has traveled a long road in the past seven years. In its journey it has enjoyed certain advantages not shared by most other area ministries. The organization is compact and its members are paid, so it has not experienced the operational problems with which volunteer groups frequently have to deal. There is no question as to who is boss, for example, and no difficulty in finding people to work on a given program. Because CENCOAD was founded for a clearly-stated purpose, moreover, it has not had to struggle to define its own identity or to work out its proper mission.

Even with advantages like these, the agency's efforts have sometimes ended in frustration. The staff worked to promote MIKOTA Opportunities, Inc., and the MID Areawide Health Planning Council. Both went under. CENCOAD experimented with educating low-income people in Sioux Falls. That had disappointing results. It has presented workshops which did no good— in a few cases, perhaps, even made a bad situation worse. Finally, about ten percent of its enablers have proved inadequate for one reason or another.

Nevertheless, the milestones along CENCOAD's way have been plentiful. The organization's staff has grown from two to eight. It has attracted grants worth 10.5 million dollars for community development projects. It has had a hand in creating 21 senior citizens' centers and a dozen youth centers. It has helped scores of small and large citizens' groups accomplish their cherished objectives. Starting with a Christian idea and an office, it has aided thousands of people in a hundred different ways.

It clearly has a long road yet to travel. While it is true that more and more people in the Basin are beginning to think in area terms, there is little evidence so far of an emerging community. We noted early on that CENCOAD has changed its original motto, "The Unit and the Unity," expressing the idea of the symbiotic community, to something more general, "People Inventing the Future Together." Building the symbiotic community has become a step toward achieving a broader objective. This shift does not imply a rejection of the symbiotic concept. It simply indicates a recognition that reconciling the needs of the unit with those of the unity is a dynamic, ongoing process rather than a process that leads to a definite, quantifiable end. The new formulation concedes the point that one cannot attain a symbiotic community. One can only attain a community in which symbiotic relationships are a major feature.

CENCOAD's staff is trying to shape a massive cultural change, to convince people to accept an unfamiliar ideal and commit themselves to it. The task might seem hopeless if the organization were not so obviously vital. Even though it cannot yet support itself through local contributions, CENCOAD has attracted enough grants and gifts to weather its 1974 financial crisis and, since the summer of 1976, has been operating in the black. Moreover, it is preparing to broaden its base of operations. Within the past year or so, a national task force of business and financial experts was formed to advise CENCOAD in exploring ways of ministering to the economic system as it has to the political. CENCOAD is vigorously inventing its own future so it can continue to help the people of the Basin invent theirs.

9. Realigning for Mission

*Regional Conferences
of the Diocese of Rochester*

The county names of upper New York State sound the area's rich heritage in a blend of English, Dutch and Indian vocabulary. Little wonder, then, that the five non-metropolitan regions of the Diocese of Rochester, which are labelled according to the counties that make them up, have names that range from the merely interesting to the poetic: Livingston-Steuben, Seneca-Cayuga, Schuyler-Chemung, Tompkins-Tioga, Yates-Ontario-Wayne. Certainly, with respect to title, these regions do not suffer from comparison with the five metropolitan regions. The latter are sections of Monroe County, where the city of Rochester is located, and they are called by the points of the compass: North, Northeast, Northwest, Southeast, Southwest.

The diocese was officially divided into regions by Bishop Joseph Hogan in February of 1972. At the same time he appointed ten priests to serve as regional coordinators. The purpose, duties and qualifications of these new officials were outlined in a document issued by the personnel board which included the following sentences: "To promote shared responsibility between parishes and to coordinate the various ministries of each region of the diocese, it is essential that in every region there be a personal representative of the ordinary of the diocese. This person, the regional coordinator, is called upon to provide the leadership and guidance that is demanded by the diocesan revitalization program launched by the Bishop and the Second Vatican Council."

These words provide the background for the decision to regionalize the diocese, a decision which had been under consideration since 1969. Regionalization was to be a tool of revitalization; it was not an end in itself. The regions were the middle rungs in a ladder which would permit better communications, both horizontal and vertical, among the various parishes and institutions within the diocese; would encourage more effective ministry on the part of those same parishes and institutions; and would serve as a framework in which church workers could support one another personally and professionally.

Have these hopes been realized? Yes, to some extent they have. On the most basic level, ten area ministry organizations now exist where in 1972 there were none. But the regionalization program has experienced many setbacks and suffered many delays. From the very beginning, it encountered widespread apathy and resistance. Reactions of this kind are largely attributable to simple inertia; regionalization called for substantial and rapid change which was unwelcome in itself. In addition, many thought the regional structures would add to the diocese's bureaucracy and drain valuable resources from the parishes without performing any useful function. These people were not convinced by the argument that the regions would not interfere with the parishes but would simply perform specialized services which were beyond the parishes' scope. They either saw no need for such services or felt that adding a new level of organization was not the way to provide them.

Regionalization was introduced into the diocese from the top without much consultation with the priests and people who were to make it a reality. But diocesan authorities still hoped that particular regional structures would be designed in part at the grassroots level and so would have a firm base of popular support. The idea was to set the process in motion, give parish leaders some ideas and then stand back and let the regions develop in response to local creativity. Little attempt was made to dictate particular forms for the regional structures or to enforce deadlines for their implementation. Each region was free to develop at its own pace and, within broad limits, in its own way.

This is the context in which the Rochester area organizations were launched. As already noted, they were intended from the beginning to be middle rungs on a diocesan ladder. In late 1970, a survey of the diocese revealed that of 192 Rochester parishes, only 65 had parish councils. The bishop was not content with this situation and, through his staff, took action to improve it. He saw the lagging development of parish councils as part of a larger problem: the inadequacy of lay participation on every level in the Church. Consequently, he directed that future councils be formed within a regional framework and that both parish and regional councils be employed to lay the groundwork for a diocesan pastoral council. A special body, the Diocesan Pastoral Council Formation Committee, was set up in May 1971 to carry out these plans.

It was on this committee's recommendation that the diocese was divided into ten regions in February 1972. As winter gave way to spring, the newly-appointed regional coordinators received a preliminary orientation to their roles and responsibilities. The bishop had established a Year of Renewal for the diocese to begin in September and the coordinators were given two goals to pursue during the course of this year. They were to promote the establishment of councils in every parish and the founding of standing committees on liturgy, education and human development in each region.

These goals took on more substance with the publication of tentative guidelines for regional "conferences," as the organizations at the regional level came to be known, in December 1972. The chief responsibilities of the conferences—by definition area ministry organizations, since they operated between parish and diocese—were to foster regional programs in the apostolate, maintain liaison with the diocesan staff departments, provide communication links between parish councils, and see to it that parish councils were formed or reorganized according to standards acceptable to the diocese.

In line with the diocese's general approach to regionalization, the guidelines were put forth as suggestions, not commands. They were also rather vague. Nowhere was it spelled out what form the regional conferences were to take, or how the coordinators might go about organizing them. As a result, very little happened in response to the guidelines. Liturgy, education and human development committees were duly set up and workshops on various topics were offered in various regions. But in March six coordinators out of ten reported that they were encountering indifference and resistance on the part of both priests and laity to the whole regional approach, and as late as December 1973, a full year after the guidelines were published, only one assembly had met in all the nonmetropolitan regions.

In April of 1973, the executive secretary of the Diocesan Pastoral Council Formation Committee resigned and the committee ceased functioning. The search for a successor prompted a fresh look at the system by which the emergence of parish councils, regional conferences and the diocesan pastoral council was being fostered and led to the conclusion that some new structure was needed. Consequently, Bishop Hogan in August established the Office of Pastoral Ministry and appointed Rev. Douglas Hoffman as its first director. Father Hoffman's job was to untangle what had become a rather confused administrative web and to integrate programs for councils with other diocesan activities.

Regionalism was not the primary concern of the Office of Pastoral Ministry (OPM), taking up only 15 percent of its time. Nevertheless, the agency's creation added an element of relative stability to the regionalization program. It was a permanent focal point to which the regional leaders could refer and from which they could expect support and aid. Among other things, OPM was responsible for convening regular meetings of the regional coordinators to exchange information, for consulting with each coordinator individually, for passing on service requests from the coordinators to the diocesan departments, for working closely with department heads in actually providing the services requested, for planning action programs that the regions and the departments could cooperate in carrying out, and for periodically reviewing the progress of each region.

Logic would seem to dictate that the greater administrative emphasis on councils and conferences would accelerate the process of their formation. On the upper and lower rungs of the diocesan ladder, this expectation was fulfilled. By early 1975, 134 of the 161 Rochester parishes and several missions had functioning councils. Father Hoffman moved quickly toward a diocesan pastoral council, too. By mid-1974, a constitution had been drafted. Parish councils and regional conferences reviewed and heavily revised this document before a final version was adopted by assemblies in most of the regions. The conferences then elected representatives to the new body from candidates submitted by the parishes and in June 1975, the diocesan pastoral council held its first meeting.

OPM was not as effective in its dealings with the middle rung of the ladder. The regions continued to develop, but with painful slowness. To some extent, the problem was caused by the resistance and inertia described earlier. By the time OPM was formed, however, the strength of the original opposition was fading. The primary reason for the continued sluggish growth of the regional conferences was a lack of coordination at or among different levels in the diocese. No one, for example, had established a system whereby one parish council could communicate and work with another on a matter of mutual concern. Thus interparish cooperation, which is the basis of sound regional programming, was weak. Also, communication between the regional coordinators and their parishes was often poor, and that between the coordinators and departmental staff was even worse.

This last problem had very severe consequences. In December 1973, eight coordinators filed reports which showed that, by and large, the diocesan departments were offering very few programs through the regional conferences. The regions, then, were not acting as effective middle-level organizations, channeling services from the diocesan level to the parish level. As a result, they lacked credibility in the eyes of the pastors and people.

These difficulties reflected the fact that the diocese had inserted a set of new structures, the regions, into a larger pattern of established structures, the departments and parishes. The newcomers had to fit in somehow; the older institutions had to make room for them, work out relationships with them. This took time and made for a good deal of confusion. No less problematic was the human dimension of the same encounter between the new and the established. Roles, identities, had to be designed for the regional coordinators, and the pastors as well as the department staff people had to decide how to behave toward them. Could a coordinator tell a pastor what to do under certain circumstances? Was a coordinator the equal of a department head, with the right to demand action on his problems? To what extent was the coordinator responsible for providing information to the departments and vice versa? Questions like these, often left open, added to the general indefiniteness which surrounded the regions and slowed their maturation. As it applied to personal relationships, this indefiniteness was also the frequent cause of misunderstandings and wounded feelings, which added yet another layer of complication.

The diocese took a number of steps to clarify its internal structure with regard to regionalization. The creation of OPM was one such step. A second was the publication of revised job descriptions for regional coordinators in April 1974. A third was the establishment of a role clarification committee with the task of defining precise functional relationships among the regional coordinators, the consultative bodies within the diocese (Priests' Council, Sisters' Council, Pastoral Council) and the departmental staff. This committee was formed in late 1973 and worked for about a year and a half, with mixed results.

Finally, in the summer of 1974, the diocese retained the services of a professional planning consultant. His responsibility was to supply a method by which all the ministry units in the diocese could define their goals and coordinate their efforts with the work of other units, so that the whole functioned smoothly and efficiently. The consultant accordingly introduced an eight-step process and the diocesan departments started working it through. But experience showed that the planning process, which had been developed in a business context, was too complex to be successfully applied in the diocese. After a year's trial, the effort was abandoned with the understanding that a simplified process would be designed for future use.

Even though the diocese was not markedly successful in dispelling the vagueness and confusion that impeded the regions' development, many significant gains were made during the 18 months following the founding of OPM. The most substantial progress occurred in the area of structural consolidation. As we have seen, education, liturgy and human development committees had been formally in existence in most regions since early 1973, and the first assemblies dated from about the same period. In addition, executive or steering committees had been widely instituted. But in many cases, these bodies were mere phantoms whose existence was more nominal than real. With one or two exceptions, the committees functioned only to request and coordinate training workshops staged by the diocesan service departments. And although the assemblies helped foster a regional consciousness by bringing concerned people together, they were in essence discussion groups rather than working parts of a ministry organization.

In the spring of 1974, OPM encouraged the coordinators to strengthen the roles of the executive committees. These bodies were to plan assembly agendas, direct the work of the standing committees and, in general, provide a controling center for all the activities of the organization. Within the next few months, the regional conferences began to show signs of greater stability. Five regions launched newsletters and, while actual ministerial programming remained minimal, the range and volume of planning activities increased steadily.

Development was further encouraged early in 1975 when OPM published a revised set of guidelines for regional conferences. (See Appendix B.) These guidelines, which will remain in force at least through mid-1977, have enabled some of the conferences at least to move beyond the organizational phase. Like the earlier set of guidelines, they are not prescriptive, and Father Hoffman himself has supported experiments which deviate from them. But they do form a starting point for the structural growth of the regional bodies and are therefore extremely influential. At present, all the conferences but one are close variations on the model they offer.

Even now, the Rochester regions are generally support-oriented; in the first years they were almost exclusively so. Support, for the most part, meant education. The diocese wanted committees, councils and conferences to emerge on the parish and regional levels, and it was necessary to train people to serve. In all the regions (though the distribution was very uneven) workshops were scheduled in a steady stream. Workshops for parish council officers became an annual affair after 1972, and there was a scattered pattern of training for religious educators, members of liturgy committees, church musicians, human development people for both parishes and regions, and so on. Departmental reports for the period from September 1974 to May 1975 showed that an average of 35 training and planning sessions were provided in each of the metropolitan regions and an average of 28 in the nonmetropolitan.

As the structure of the regional conferences became progressively more firm and the need for training become somewhat less urgent, action programs began to appear. As early as March 1975, the executive committee of the Northwest region openly opposed the closing of part of a local hospital and the human development committee in the Livingston-Steuben region helped set up a three-parish cooperative food pantry. At about the same time, planning began in the Southeast region for a major project: the rehabilitation of owner-occupied homes belonging to needy families.

The past year has seen the launching of a number of other action ministries. The liturgy committee of the Chemung-Schuyler region involved over 100 people in making arrangements for a diocesan-wide Chrism Mass in the spring. Two regions have started groups for separated, widowed and divorced Catholics with good results. The first meeting of one of the groups drew 80 persons. And the diocese has recently returned a percentage of the money collected through a hunger appeal to the regions for their own use. It will be up to the coordinators or the human development committees to spend these funds—they total $1000 in some cases—to stimulate local action on the world hunger problem.

The observer can get a fairly clear notion of the development of the regions' capacity to operate apostolic programs by tracing the history of the nursing home question. In November 1973, a diocesan task force was appointed to gauge the adequacy of Catholic religious services to these institutions. After three months, it recommended upgrading nursing home ministry in several specific ways. The Priests' Council approved the task force's recommendations and a decision was made to implement them through the regions. To this end, the task force drew up a detailed plan for training sessions in a particular "pilot" region. This training was carried out and eventually offered in three other regions as well, and it appeared that the renewed ministry was well begun.

But a second report filed a year later noted that, while individual parishes had improved their services to nursing homes, no comprehensive approach to the problem had yet emerged. Obviously, the regions had not taken unified action as regions; what response there was was scattered and uncoordinated. The task force recommended that minimum standards for nursing home ministry be defined that could be uniformly applied throughout the diocese.

Such standards were accordingly adopted late in 1975, and Bishop Hogan asked the regional coordinators to see that they were implemented. When the coordinators reported back in June of 1976, though, only basic sacramental services were being provided. OPM had offered no active leadership and the regional conferences as a whole were still too weak to administer a developed program involving the cooperation of nearly all the parishes. Presently, a new effort is underway. The responsibility for seeing that the standards for nursing home ministry are fulfilled is still in the hands of the regional coordinators. But OPM has taken steps to assure closer communications between the coordinators and local pastors and has encouraged pastors to cooperate with the program. Father Hoffman has also suggested certain methods for getting the job done—working through the human development committee, for example—in meetings with the coordinators. The hope is that success in this major action project with diocesan help will make it possible for the regions to succeed without diocesan help in the future.

While the regional conferences have been struggling with the difficulties of running action programs, they have been gaining greater effectiveness in terms of giving support and advice. The workshops offered through the regions may be less frequent than in the past, but experience has enabled those conducting them to provide better focussed material. The advisory function now works in three ways. First, the diocese can consult with the regional conferences. The task force on Confirmation, for example, asked the Northeast assembly to react to certain ideas in January 1976. Second, the conferences can give unsolicited opinions or make unsolicited recommendations to the diocese on issues of their choosing. In December 1975, the Southeast assembly submitted a series of proposals to the diocesan pastoral council aimed at making all church buildings accessible to the handicapped. The proposals were readily accepted. More recently, two other regions have recommended that all decisions on the diocesan level which could affect parish budgets be published before a certain date, and that the diocese take some firm positions regarding inner-city ministry. Third, the conferences can exert influence in a downward direction, to the parishes within their territories. The program by which the nursing home ministry standards are implemented will almost certainly involve advice-giving of this kind.

Support, advice, action: the Rochester regional conference seems to cover a great deal of ground. In theory, it certainly does. The conferences are among the relatively few area ministry organizations whose missions are entirely general; according to the diocesan guidelines, they do not even have a dominant function. At present, they are all support groups that also perform advisory and action ministries, but that is an accident of growth. In five years, it is likely that the support function will fade into the background in some of them, to be replaced by either advice or action.

Since nearly all the conferences are variations on the model presented in the 1975 guidelines, it is to the guidelines that we must look for a basic understanding of how these organizations work. The responsibilities of the conferences are defined quite broadly. The regional conference is "a forum for speaking, [listening] and active sharing as Church. . . ." It exists to promote cooperation among all the parishes and institutions of the region and to coordinate the ministries that arise from such cooperation. It may also generate ministries and operate them through its own resources. It stands pledged to work with other diocesan groups such as the pastoral council and the staff departments. Finally, the conference must elect delegates to the pastoral council and pass along any proposals and requests that its member parishes and institutions may suggest.

The regional conference is an organization made up of other organizations within the diocesan framework. Those who attend meetings do not speak for themselves, as individuals, but rather are representatives of the parishes and institutions of the region. Membership is not voluntary but mandatory. By decision of the bishop, every parish and institution must belong to the conference so that, ideally at least, the region can act as a unit in planning and carrying out its work.

The structure of the conference is fairly simple. At the top is the regional coordinator, appointed by the bishop as his personal representative in the region. He serves as chairman of the executive committee and convener of the assembly. He is also responsible for maintaining adequate communications between the conference on the one hand and the bishop and the diocesan departments on the other. As his title states, the coordinator is expected to retain an overview of the whole conference and do his best to assure that its various components work together.

The executive committee, as noted earlier, is the control center for the conference. It is made up of the coordinator, any associate coordinators he may appoint, the chairmen of the standing ministry committees and others; in general, anyone in a position of authority in the conference is likely to find a place on this body. The committee has three principal functions. As the agenda committee for the assembly, it determines what comes before that group and, just as importantly, which agencies and institutions may submit items for the assembly's consideration. It is also responsible for ensuring that the members of the assembly understand clearly what is presented to them and what is expected of them, and it handles the administrative work connected with assembly meetings. As a steering group for the ministry committees, the executive committee sees to it that these groups meet and that they have the budget and the access to staff necessary to do their work. It accepts reports from the ministry committees and offers guidance to them. As the communications link between the conference and the parishes in the region, the executive committees may publish a newsletter. Whether it does or not, it will always make sure that local pastors and parish councils are aware of the important plans and programs occupying the conference at any given time.

The assembly is a grassroots body composed of delegates from each parish and institution in the area. Its basic function is to serve as a forum in which the ministerial needs of the region are identified, articulated and set in an order of priority. Once this process is complete, the assembly becomes a direct advisory body, urging groups outside itself to take action on the needs it has surfaced. These groups range from local parish councils through the regional ministry committees to the diocesan pastoral council and diocesan agencies. Besides fulfilling this primary responsibility, the assembly has two secondary jobs. It annually approves the objectives of the ministerial committees and it provides a means by which the bishop and diocesan-level groups can consult with the grassroots.

The last of the regional conference components, the ministerial committees, form the action arm of the organization. In addition to maintaining the standard committees for liturgy, religious education and human development, a few regions cover other areas like youth and family life as well. The ministerial committees may identify needs and pass them on to the assembly for confirmation, with the understanding that the assembly will refer them back afterward. In other words, they may originate their own projects. Or they may simply respond to the suggestions of the executive committee and the assembly. In either case, they will spend the bulk of their time actually operating programs in the apostolate, programs which seek to deal directly with some regional need or which help local parishes do a better job.

This is the theoretical outline of the Rochester regional conferences. "Outline" is the correct term because, even though the guidelines describe the chief organizational elements in some depth, much is left to individual choice and interpretation. For example, how is the executive committee to operate? By majority vote? Collegially, under the leadership of the regional coordinator? On the authority of the coordinator? Because of the power invested in the executive committee, the answer to this question could determine not only the style but the very nature of a particular conference. In the same way, the guidelines do not specify how often the various components of the conference must meet. Remaining within the guidelines, then, the people of a given region could create a loosely coordinated, slow-moving organization or a fast-paced, integrated, dynamic one.

Since no rigid standard was imposed, different regional conferences have developed in somewhat different directions. In order to get a feel for the reality of these organizations, we must let all that has been said so far about the history and structure of the conferences serve as background for the concrete examination of a single region. Our focus, of course, is on rural ministry, and the most successful nonmetropolitan organization in the diocese to date has been the Tompkins-Tioga Regional Conference.

Like all the other rural regions, Tompkins-Tioga was slow to jell and made little headway for the first two years of its existence. The two counties stretch about 40 miles north to south and about 25 east to west. It was hard to get priests and people from the 14 parishes of the region together for meetings to establish a structure for the conference and set it in motion. Moreover, Tompkins-Tioga is at the far end of the diocese from Rochester, which complicated communications with the regional coordinator's only source of information and advice. Everything had to be handled either by letter or by long-distance phone. These problems of distance were aggravated by the nature of the territory, which is perhaps the most rural of all the Rochester regions. The services offered by the diocesan departments were typically designed with an urban context in mind and therefore had limited applicability in Tompkins-Tioga.

Nevertheless, once the structure of the conference was intact it functioned rather well. In the summer of 1974, the first regional newsletter appeared. It announced a regional religious education workshop, a youth ministry workshop for the Tioga County parishes and the availability of training sessions for parish liturgy committee personnel. It also announced the date of the first regional assembly and added that the delegates would weigh approval of the regional conference constitution and the constitution of the diocesan pastoral council. In September, a second newsletter appeared giving notice of still other educational opportunities. And on October 17, the assembly did meet and approve the two constitutions. (The Tompkins-Tioga Constitution will be found in Appendix B.)

The Tompkins-Tioga constitution follows the design presented in the OPM guidelines rather closely. The statement of purpose mentions support, advisory and action functions, and all the components of the organization are described in substantially the same way as in the guidelines. There are some significant changes, however. Support occupies a more central place than it does in the model. Potential curbs are set on the power of the regional coordinator by a stipulation that he need not be the chairman of the executive committee. The officers of the assembly sit on the executive committee, which has the effect of making the former less a stepchild of the latter. Finally, the role of the ministerial committees is stated more in terms of coordination and communication than action. In sum, although it is still an organization in which the popular assembly has little power, the Tompkins-Tioga conference makes more concessions to democratic principles than the model of the guidelines does. Its constitution also articulates more fully the role of the conference as a connecting link between parish and diocese.

Immediately after the regional constitution was adopted, the Tompkins-Tioga newsletter stopped appearing for two full years. Surprisingly, this did not prevent the growth of a regional consciousness, which was well advanced by late 1975. It was fostered for the most part by a regular schedule of priests' meetings. Through these meetings, the clergy became accustomed to the idea of cooperation across parish lines and so were in a position to provide effective leadership when region-wide efforts were launched. The presence of an active executive committee also promoted the emergence of a sense of region. Not only did the committee move to identify the needs of the region and propose ways of dealing with them, its members paid personal visits to each parish in the fall of 1975. They were thus able to gain firsthand knowledge of how the priests and their parish councils felt on selected issues. At the same time, they communicated their concern that each pastor and each council see themselves as integral parts of the region.

Most of the Conference's activities have centered around education. During 1975, some parishes were grouped into clusters to mitigate the problem of distance and to take advantage of any long-standing ties or sympathies among neighboring congregations. Diocesan staff gave several workshops for committee members in the parishes of these clusters. Then in May 1976, the region sponsored a day-long workshop for pastors and assistant pastors that aimed at giving them the skills to work more effectively with their parish councils and committees. People from the conference initiated this program, planned it and recruited Father Hoffman, representatives of the diocesan education, liturgy and human development departments and an expert on group dynamics from Cornell University to make the presentations. The workshop was well received, and as a result the conference leadership set up another one for the fall. It formed the major component of the regional assembly meeting. The emphasis was on the authority of the parish council, a topic that was covered through a talk by an invited speaker, a panel presentation and small group discussion.

These educational programs, like the priests' meetings, essentially provide support. They have been supplemented in the Tompkins-Tioga region by nascent efforts in the advisory and action fields. Recently, the diocesan pastoral council passed and sent on to Bishop Hogan a proposal from the conference that any diocesan policy which would affect parish budgets be promulgated by a certain date each year. As far as action is concerned, the conference formed a committee in the spring of 1976 to carry out the bishop's wish that all parish council constitutions be reviewed to determine their conformity with diocesan guidelines. By September, eight of the 14 parishes had complied. Also, the coordinator wrote to all nursing home administrators in the region explaining the minimum ministry standards the diocese had adopted and asking for information on the services they were presently receiving. This is a first step in the campaign, mentioned earlier, to bring the long discussion over nursing home ministry to a successful close. Finally, a World Hunger Committee has been set up to use funds returned to the regions by the diocese in the wake of a special hunger appeal. This committee, so far, has conducted a poster contest and will display the winning entries in business places to increase popular consciousness of the world food crisis.

In terms of the development of a sense of regional identity, Tompkins-Tioga is the equal of any conference in the diocese, including the metropolitan ones. It may be less advanced than a few regions with regard to programs, but if so the difference is not great. Tompkins-Tioga, then, can stand as a fair illustration of how far regionalization in the Diocese of Rochester has progressed since its beginnings nearly five years ago. The conference is a functioning area organization with a complete structure and the capacity to provide support, to give advice or to engage in action. Its real activities, however, are spotty and undramatic. They range from solid support programs to extremely simple advisory and action efforts, and are in general heavily dependent on diocesan staff. As a ministry organization, Tompkins-Tioga is in a period of transition. It is past the formative stage, but has not yet attained the maturity to pursue its own independent apostolate.

To many, five years will seem a very long time to produce so undeveloped an organization as Tompkins-Tioga. Diocesan officials have given considerable thought to the question of timing. In the beginning, as we have seen, they decided to adopt an unassertive approach toward the regions. Hoping to see the conferences emerge as products of grassroots creativity, they avoided imposing their will on priests and people. Recently however, this policy, at least in its extreme form, has come into question. Some argue that the regions have not been given enough firm leadership and support. The conferences would probably have matured more quickly, for example, had funding been available earlier to initiate programs. But they received nothing from the diocese until June 1975 and only $1000 per year afterward.

This new perspective has led to changes in the diocese's dealings with the regions. Father Hoffman recognizes that too slow a pace threatens the ultimate success of the program; momentum can be sustained for only so long in the absence of strong positive results. Within the past few months, he and his staff have begun to direct more of their attention toward the conferences. Father was in the habit of meeting five or six times a year with the regional coordinators as a group. Now he meets with each man individually on a rotating basis for planning and evaluation. These consultations ensure close contact between the coordinators and the diocese and give them a chance to get help in making difficult decisions.

OPM has instituted more definite controls over the work of the conferences and is attempting to streamline the procedures by which they operate. One example of these controls is the new approach, discussed earlier, which OPM has taken to the fulfillment of the minimum standards for nursing home ministry. A second is the return of funds collected during the hunger appeal. By placing this money in the hands of the conferences and demanding an accounting of how it is spent, the diocese is forcing the regional structures to function and to gain experience in ministry.

As far as procedures are concerned, OPM is aiming to improve the performance of the regional assemblies. Ideally, the assemblies act as communications links between the parishes on the one hand and the diocese and various action groups on the other. Parish representatives discuss certain issues and their conclusions are passed on for further study or implementation. This system can only work, however, if the executive committee of the conference fulfills its responsibility to make up a proper agenda for assembly meetings and distributes it in advance. Once they have an agenda, the delegates can confer with the pastor and council of their parishes and come to the meeting armed with the parish's official viewpoint on the matters under consideration. Otherwise, they can do little more than give a personal opinion. Father Hoffman hopes to get these institutional connections operating smoothly so the conferences' value as middle structures in the diocese can be more fully realized.

As they address the future, the regions represent a unique opportunity for the Diocese of Rochester. The most important fact about these new structures is that the ministry they offer links and supplements the ministry of parish and diocese. Their reason for existence is that a gap, some uncovered territory, stretches between the two. The area ministry organization here, as elsewhere, has not arisen as a substitute for older institutions that have outlived their usefulness. It fits into a well-established system, making that system more effective by increasing the range and quality of services it can deliver.

On November 28, 1975, Bishop Hogan issued a pastoral letter entitled *You Are Living Stones*. In it he projects a vision of the diocese as a vital body in which all the parts cooperate in the pursuit of a single goal, the service of Christ. This is the vision behind the creation of the regional conferences. They are tools, only partly useful as yet, but potentially able to weld the diocese, top and bottom, into a unified whole. If the struggle to reach this goal is a difficult one, the goal itself seems worth the effort. A season of promise lies beyond what Father Hoffman calls, in a curious but striking metaphor, "the long winter of our renewal."

APPENDIX A: DEFINITIONS

AREA MINISTRY ORGANIZATION: an organization for Christian ministry structured at a level higher than a parish and lower than a diocese (or judicatory)

> May be denominational or ecumenical. May be simple or complex, formally or informally organized (for example, a group, committee, agency, assembly, council, institution or association). May perform support functions, advisory functions, action functions or any combination thereof.

RURAL AREA MINISTRY ORGANIZATION: one that operates wholly or largely in open countryside or in towns of 10,000 or less, away from cities, suburbs and urban fringes

SUPPORT AREA MINISTRY ORGANIZATION: an area association of church workers whose sole or principal function is to provide personal and/or professional support to its members in their lives and work

ADVISORY AREA MINISTRY ORGANIZATION: an area organization whose sole or principal function is to influence policy and encourage other units within the Church to undertake programs in the apostolate

> May advise parishes, the diocese or other church agencies and groups. May make recommendations on its own initiative and/or respond to requests. May be made up of parishes, individuals, dioceses or their agencies, other church institutions and groups, or any combination thereof. Membership may be voluntary or mandated by church authority.

ACTION AREA MINISTRY ORGANIZATION: an area organization whose sole or principal function is to operate apostolic programs that strengthen or complement parish programs

> May operate generalized and/or highly specialized ministries. May be established to conduct designated programs and/or to take up any challenge to which the members desire to respond. Membership may be voluntary or mandated by church authority.
>
> *Interparish Program:* an association of two or more parishes engaged in action area ministry, either through a cooperative structure made up of delegates from the member parishes or through a "part for the whole" agreement whereby one parish administers a program in the name of all
>
> *Interparish Staff:* an association of two or more parishes whose staffs engage in action area ministry, either merging into one staff (closely integrated type) or retaining their separate identities while sharing work (loosely integrated type)
>
> *Other:* a parish, organization, diocese or diocesan agency; or an association of individuals, dioceses or their agencies, other church institutions and groups or any combination thereof; or an association of any of the above with parishes, engaged in action area ministry

**APPENDIX B: SAMPLE
CONSTITUTION AND GUIDELINES**

GUIDELINES OF THE TOWN AND COUNTRY APOSTOLIC
COUNCIL
IN THE ARCHDIOCESE OF LOUISVILLE / April 1974

NAME. The name of this organization shall be Town and Country Apostolic (TACA) Council.

PURPOSE. The purpose of TACA Council shall be to support fellowship among the various ministers serving the Town and Country Apostolate, in order to establish mutual sharing and more effective ministry.

MEMBERSHIP. The TACA Council shall be composed of voluntary membership of persons interested in the Town and Country Apostolate of the Archdiocese of Louisville.

A $5.00 membership fee due annually in January shall determine active membership with voting and office holding rights. A $2.00 associate membership fee allows one to receive all TACA mailings, but no voting or office holding rights.

OFFICES. There shall be an elected President, Vice President, Secretary, Treasurer, and four members of the Board of Directors.

PRESIDENT. Nominations for the office of President shall be made at the regular TACA Council meeting in October of the odd-numbered years, where nominations shall be reduced to two by a simple plurality vote of the members present. If a nomination is refused, the next highest plurality vote shall determine the nominee.

The President shall be elected by a majority of votes cast by the members present and by the certified absentee ballots at the regular TACA Council meeting in November.

Term of office shall be for two years with the possibility of reelection for no more than one more consecutive term.

The President and Board shall prepare the agenda, notify all members of the agenda, set the meeting date, time and place and notify all members.

The President shall select and appoint such persons as chairmen of standing and *ad hoc* committees as he so desires.

The President shall be *ex officio* Chairman of the Board of Directors of the TACA Council.

The President is empowered to act and speak in the name of the TACA Council membership when he actually has a mandate or when he can, in emergency, obtain a consensus of the Board of Directors.

The President shall appoint any member as Treasurer should that office be vacated before the elected term of office.

VICE PRESIDENT. Nomination and election of the Vice President shall be made in the same manner as that of the President in the even-numbered years.

The Vice President shall assume the office of President should that office be vacated.

The Vice President presides in the absence of the President.

SECRETARY. The Secretary shall be elected the same year and in the same manner as the President (odd-numbered years).

The Secretary shall keep minutes of all meetings.

The Secretary is responsible for public relations.

The Secretary shall be responsible for news releases to the press.

TREASURER. The Treasurer shall be nominated and elected in the same manner as the Vice President and for the same term (even-numbered years).

The Treasurer shall keep all financial records and transact all financial business of the TACA Council.

BOARD OF DIRECTORS. There are four regular members of the Board of Directors with the four elected officers its *ex officio* members.

The Board shall be nominated and elected in the same manner as the President one meeting later than election of the President.

The Board of Directors' term of office shall be for two years. Two shall be elected in the odd-numbered years and two shall be elected in the even-numbered years.

Elected members of the Board of Directors may be reelected for only one more consecutive term.

The Board of Directors shall hold meetings monthly before each regular meeting.

In an emergency, when the TACA Council members cannot be called to a meeting, the Board of Directors shall be empowered to advise the President on the will of the majority of the membership.

Special meetings may be called by a majority of the members of the Board.

COUNCIL MEETINGS. Meetings shall be held each month, excluding July and August. Special meetings may be called by t he President with a majority of the Board Members. A quorum of paid membership ($5.00) is necessary for any decision-making or voting.

Meetings shall always begin with or end with a worship service.

Date, time and agenda of meetings shall be set by the Board.

CHANGES. Changes in the *Guidelines* of the TACA Council may be executed by a reading of the proposed change at a regular meeting of the TACA Council and by a majority vote of the members present at the next regular meeting following the proposal reading.

CONSTITUTION OF THE DEANERY THREE COUNCIL
OF THE DIOCESE OF TULSA / July 11, 1976

NAME. The name of this organization shall be the Deanery Three Council of the Roman Catholic Diocese of Tulsa, hereinafter referred to as "Deanery."

PURPOSE. Our purpose is to be an advocacy, advisory and forum group which focuses on the Church's mission which we believe to be: preaching the gospel to and nourishing the Faith of the Catholic Community in whatever circumstances we find them; growing in Christ with other Christians; sharing faith and fellowship with the unchurched and those with no religious affiliation; transforming the social order to God's intended purpose; and supporting the diocesan, national and worldwide ministries of the Church.

We believe that it is Christ who works through us and hope that by gathering in His name, listening to His word and seeking His wisdom in prayer we will ". . .enjoy the increased consolation of the Holy Spirit . . ." (Acts 9:31), by providing fellowship and recreation, aiding personal and spiritual development, providing opportunities for education and providing an occasion for the reinforcement of Christian values.

We advocate and advise on the need for programs or policies, but do not ourselves operate such programs or policies. We serve as both a forum for the exchange of information and as the occasion for members and others to initiate cooperative efforts independently of the Deanery.

MEMBERSHIP. Any practicing Catholic who is a member of a deanery parish and who is chosen by a due process agreed upon by that parish shall be eligible for membership on the Deanery. All pastors of deanery parishes shall by merit of their assignment be members of the Deanery.

Any professional lay or religious church workers, other than pastors, shall be non-voting, consulting members of the Deanery.

Lay delegates and alternates may be chosen by parish council selection, a vote of the parish, selection by the pastor, or by any combination of the three. Each parish and mission is entitled to two lay delegates and two alternates.

Any pastor, delegate and/or alternate of a deanery parish or mission, diocesan council delegates and/or their alternates and any interested persons may attend Deanery meetings.

When a vacancy occurs in a parish's delegation, that parish should by its own process and within thirty days of the occurrence of the vacancy select another delegate whose name shall be submitted to the deanery President.

A President and Vice President shall be elected by the Deanery from its own membership. Their terms of office shall be two years. A Treasurer shall be selected by the Dean from the deanery membership, subject to the approval of the Deanery. The Treasurer's term of office will be two years.

The Executive Committee of the Deanery shall be composed of the Dean, the elected officers of the Deanery and the Treasurer. Their duties shall be limited to those specified in this Constitution.

The President shall preside at all meetings of the Deanery, using Robert's Rules of Order unless otherwise specified in this Constitution. In addition, he shall be a member of all committees.

The Vice President shall preside at all meetings in the absence of the President and shall act as an assistant to the President and under his or her direction.

It shall be the duty of the Treasurer to prepare the two yearly financial reports of the Deanery. In addition, the Treasurer shall be responsible for the billing of all accounts receivable and the countersigning of all checks.

The Executive Committee shall act in the name of the Deanery when a meeting of the full Deanery is not expedient. All decisions of the Executive Committee shall be subject to review by the full Deanery.

It shall be the duty of the Executive Secretary to perform the following: publication and mailing of minutes prior to each meeting; preparation of all correspondence approved by the Deanery; duplication of all materials for deanery delegates; preparation of yearly budget proposal for approval by Deanery; and payment of all bills and signing of all checks.

The Recording Secretary shall take the minutes at each meeting and draft them for publication. A person, not a member of the Deanery, shall be appointed for this position by the President.

MEETINGS. Meetings should be held at least every two months. The date of the following meeting will be set at the end of each regular meeting.

A preliminary agenda for the next meeting will be set at the end of each regular meeting. Items can be added to the agenda by notifying the President at least ten days prior to the meeting at which they are to be considered. In urgent cases an addition to the agenda can be made at the beginning of a meeting with the consent of the members present. A copy of the agenda, with the minutes, should be mailed to each delegate at least a week before a meeting.

The President may call a special meeting with the approval of the Executive Committee. The President and the Executive Committee will set the agenda. A notice of the special meeting must be in the mail ten days prior to the meeting.

VOTING. Each duly chosen delegate shall be entitled to one vote. In case of absence, his or her alternate may vote. At their option a total vote may be divided fractionally among a parish's delegation. Proxy votes may be cast when a signed proxy statement is presented to the President.

BUDGETING. An annual budget shall be proposed to the Deanery by the Executive Secretary at the first meeting after January 15 of each year. The proportionate amount of funding requested from each member parish or mission shall be based on the ACDO figures of the previous year. This will give each member parish or mission sufficient time to accept financial participation for inclusion in its fiscal year budget. In the event financial participation of member parish(es) or mission(s) would not be approved by parish council(s), the Deanery may seek other means of providing funding for Deanery activities.

The Treasurer shall give a financial report on income, expenses and current balance of all financial matters which have taken place since the last report at the first meeting after July 1 and at the first meeting after January 1 of each year.

DELEGATES TO THE DIOCESAN PASTORAL COUNCIL. The deanery shall elect the necessary number of persons to serve as delegates to the diocesan pastoral council. Such election shall be held no later than November 30 of each year. A nominating committee whose membership shall be no less than three persons, being restricted to deanery delegates, shall be appointed or selected by the President at least thirty days prior to the voting on such delegate(s). A nominee for diocesan pastoral council delegate may be any member of a parish or mission within the deanery boundaries.

No more than one diocesan pastoral council delegate shall be from any single parish or mission.

Should the diocesan pastoral council delegate not be a member of the Deanery, that delegate shall become a voting member of the Deanery.

The term of office for a diocesan pastoral council delegate shall be three years. The delegate is limited to two consecutive terms.

REVIEWING, AMENDING, RATIFYING. This Constitution shall be reviewed annually. Such review shall be made no sooner than six months nor later than ten months after its initial adoption, and each succeeding year thereafter within thirty days of the anniversary date of the last review.

Any article of this Constitution may be amended by a vote of the Deanery members at a regular meeting. Proposed amendments shall be considered at the meeting in which they appear on the agenda. Passage of any amendment shall be valid only if sixty percent or more of the voting members present at the meeting vote in favor of the amendment. No amendment shall be adopted with less than six votes.

If after reviewing this Constitution there are no proposed amendments, then this Constitution shall be ratified by a simple majority of delegates present.

CONSTITUTION OF THE INTERCHURCH COORDINAT-ING COUNCIL
OF WEST-CENTRAL MISSOURI / September 3, 1970

PREAMBLE. We, the representatives of several religious bodies serving the communities in West-Central Missouri, each motivated by his own religious convictions, find that we share a common concern for the lives of the people in our area, a common commitment to serve our God by serving the people He created and a common desire to act out our concerns for people by becoming involved with the problems of our society. We seek to establish lines for effective communication and collective study, planning and action. The wide diversity of religious backgrounds we represent is an exciting and meaningful opportunity to add new dimensions to our individual attempts to speak to our society through shared ideas and plans. We believe that speaking with one voice when our individual consciences permit can be much more effective at times than independent action.

We, therefore, commit our resources for creative leadership, seek to gain the commitment of religious bodies and other groups and individuals that share our concerns to join us in an organization for collective research, planning and action aimed at the changing character of our area and the social problems and adjustments that may become evident from time to time.

NAME. The name of this organization shall be "Interchurch Coordinating Council of West-Central Missouri, Incorporated," and is incorporated under the General Not For Profit Corporation Act, Revised Statutes of Missouri.

PURPOSE. The four basic purposes of the Council are:

Communication. The Council is a listening agency, an arena for the exchange of ideas and a channel for communication among and between religious bodies, agencies, other interest groups and individuals in our society. We invite and listen to the concerns of individuals and groups who live in our area, so that together we may attempt to identify real needs and bring them to the attention of those who are inclined toward or committed to becoming involved.

Coordination. The Council is a coordinating agency, bringing together the individuals and groups whose training, ability and interest equip them for service so that together they may study, plan and act. It serves as an agency to coordinate the resources, the experts, the professionals and the concerned in general.

Planning. The Council is an agency equipped for the discipline of long-range planning and a resource for providing leadership for task force groups who want to identify needs as they emerge, to collect data, to engage in organized research, to give direction when called for to task groups and to evaluate each project.

People Participation. The Council is an action starter. As individual concerns emerge and are identified, it provides the necessary framework, resources and leadership so that those whose interests and commitments dictate involvement may act together. It encourages the widest possible participation, but is always committed to a respect for those who feel that their distinctive witness or approach is best maintained by separate action.

MEMBERSHIP. Membership in the Council shall be open to religious bodies on a judicatory level, to individual congregations, and to individuals.

ORGANIZATIONAL STRUCTURE. The Council shall be structured to include a Cabinet, an Assembly and various Task Force groups.

The *Cabinet* shall be a body of representatives of the member groups that form the Council. The Cabinet shall be the decision-making body of the Council. It shall conduct the Council's business, direct the staff and be responsible for the administration of all the Council's affairs. The objectives of the Cabinet shall be those set forth in the statement of purpose of this Constitution. The Cabinet shall meet as established by Bylaws.

The *Assembly* shall be a representative body, composed of delegates from member church groups. The Assembly shall be advisory to the Cabinet. The responsibilities of the Assembly shall be as specified in the Bylaws of this organization.

Task Force Groups may be certified by the Cabinet to study and work on particular interests or concerns shared by two or more members of the Council.

Executive Committee. The Cabinet may establish an executive committee, whose responsibilities are set forth in the Bylaws of this organization.

Executive Director. The Cabinet may employ and/or contract for an executive director.

AMENDMENTS. This Constitution may be amended at any regular meeting of the Cabinet, provided written notice of the meeting and a copy of the proposed amendment shall have been given at least two weeks prior to the meeting; and that two-thirds affirmative vote of the members present and voting on the amendment be recorded.

AMENDMENT 1. The Council as a legal entity may provide the corporate structure for task forces when this is required to fulfill their responsibilities or goals.

BYLAWS OF THE INTERCHURCH COORDINATING COUNCIL OF WEST-CENTRAL MISSOURI / September 3, 1970

MEMBERSHIP. Membership in the Council shall be open to religious bodies on a judicatory level, to individual congregations, to individuals and to other qualified organizations as set forth in the Constitution. Judicatory level membership shall be open to church organizations immediately above the local congregation (e.g., district, presbytery, diocese, etc.). Congregation and individual membership is open to those whose judicatories have not elected to participate in the Council.

Member bodies shall be entitled to delegates in the Cabinet and Assembly. Each member judicatory shall be permitted one delegate to the Cabinet and such proportionate representation in the Assembly as may be established by action of the Cabinet. Member congregations not supported by judicatory membership shall caucus by denominations to elect a delegate to the Cabinet and shall have proportionate representation in the Assembly as may be established by action of the Cabinet. Other affiliated organizations shall be entitled to one delegate to the Cabinet and such representation in the Assembly as may be established by the Cabinet.

Individuals and organizations other than religious bodies may, by action of the Cabinet, be invited to membership because of interrelated interests or special resources.

FINANCIAL COMMITMENT. Member judicatories and member congregations shall be asked to support the Council financially on a per member basis.

STRUCTURE. The basic structure of the Council shall include a Cabinet, an Assembly, and various Task Force Groups.

The *Cabinet* shall be the decision-making body of the Council. It shall be a body of representatives of the member groups that form the Council. It shall conduct the Council's business, direct the staff and be responsible for the administration of all the Council's affairs. It shall elect the officers of the Council from among its members; they shall be a Moderator, Vice-Moderator, Secretary and Treasurer. It shall establish a budget for the current fiscal year. The Cabinet shall be the Board of Directors of the corporation, and its officers shall be the officers of the corporation.

The Assembly shall be advisory to the Cabinet. It shall consist of proportionate representation of member bodies, as established by the Cabinet. It shall review the programs of the Council and offer its evaluation and suggestions. It shall serve as a channel of communication between the Council and member bodies and within the membership. It shall express the concerns of the groups and individuals its members represent.

Task Force Groups are the action arm of the Council. They shall be certified by the Cabinet to study and work on particular interests or concerns, or concerns shared by two or more members of the Council. They shall organize themselves and meet at will. They shall speak and act only for those who compose them, and not for the Council as a whole. They shall have access to the resources and advice of the Cabinet.

The *Executive Committee* shall be composed of the officers of the Cabinet and the Executive Director, *ex officio*. It conducts the business of the Council between Cabinet meetings. It reviews the financial condition of the Council and makes regular reports to the Cabinet. It recommends action for consideration of the Cabinet. All actions of the Executive Committee are subject to review and action of the Cabinet.

The *Executive Director* shall be the administrative officer. He shall oversee the conduct and operation of the office. He shall prepare recommendations for consideration of the Executive Committee and Cabinet. He shall work with Task Force Groups to assist in the accomplishment of their goals. He shall undertake study and research on behalf of the Council. He shall represent the Council in various inter-church and ecumenical relationships. He shall be an *ex officio* member of all committees, task force groups, etc.

ELECTIONS. Not less than thirty days prior to the annual election the Moderator shall appoint, with the approval of the Cabinet, a nominating committee of not less than three members.

The nominating committee shall select nominees for expiring terms. No officer shall be eligible for the same office for more than two full consecutive terms.

Additional names may be placed in nomination at the time of balloting from the floor.

At the annual election there shall be elected a Moderator, Vice-Moderator, Secretary and a Treasurer.

Voting shall be by individual cabinet members and no person shall cast more than one ballot. Proxies will not be recognized.

Officers shall take office January 1, which date shall begin the Council's fiscal year.

All officers shall be elected for one year.

MEETINGS. The annual election meeting of the Cabinet shall be held in December and notice of such meeting shall be mailed to each Cabinet member at least fourteen days prior thereto.

The Cabinet shall hold regular bi-monthly meetings on such dates as may be set.

Special meetings may be called by the Moderator as needed. A special meeting must be called if at least three Cabinet members request it.

Regular meetings of the Executive Committee shall be set by the Moderator. Date, time, and place shall be public information.

The Council Assembly shall hold semi-annual meetings, the dates and places to be set by the Cabinet.

No meeting of the Cabinet shall be recognized unless a quorum of the Cabinet members is present. One-third of the membership of the Cabinet shall constitute a quorum.

DUTIES OF OFFICERS. *Moderator.* The Moderator shall be the chief executive officer of the Council. He shall preside over all meetings of the Cabinet. He shall have general and active management of the business of the Cabinet and shall see that all orders and resolutions of the Cabinet are carried out. He shall be an *ex officio* member of all committees and shall have the general powers and duties of supervision and management vested in the office of president.

Vice-Moderator. The Vice-Moderator shall perform the duties and exercise the powers of the Moderator during the absence or disability of the Moderator. He shall represent the Moderator and share in the general management of the Cabinet at the discretion of the Moderator. In the event that the office of Moderator becomes vacant, the Vice-Moderator shall assume the office and a successor to the Vice-Moderator shall be elected. The Vice-Moderator shall serve as Moderator for the remainder of his predecessor's term.

Secretary. The Secretary shall attend the meetings of the Cabinet and shall preserve in books of the Council the true minutes of the proceedings of all such meetings, shall be the custodian of the Council records and in general shall perform such duties as are incident to the office of the Secretary.

Treasurer. The Treasurer shall oversee the disposition of funds and securities of the Council. He shall give his report at all regular meetings of the Cabinet or Council Assembly, and in general perform all the duties incident to the office of Treasurer. He shall issue checks, drafts and orders for payment of money, which shall be countersigned by the Moderator or Executive Director. He shall deposit funds of the Corporation not otherwise employed in Union State Bank in Clinton, Missouri, or such other depositories as the Cabinet shall designate by resolution.

Executive Director. The Executive Director shall be charged with the responsibility of executive of Council business. He shall report to the Cabinet at regular meetings. The authority to engage subordinate personnel shall normally be delegated to the Executive Director and they shall be responsible to him.

RULES OF ORDER. Robert's Rules of Order Revised shall be used at the discretion of the chairman to govern the proceedings at meetings. They must be used if requested by any member.

AMENDMENTS. These Bylaws may be amended by a two-thirds vote of members present and voting at any general or special meeting, provided written notice of the proposed action has been given to each Cabinet member at his last known address at least ten days prior thereto.

BYLAWS OF THE MORGAN-SCOTT PROJECT FOR CO-OPERATIVE CHRISTIAN CONCERNS IN EASTERN TENNESSEE/ January 26, 1974

NAME. The name of this organization is the Morgan-Scott Project for Cooperative Christian Concerns.

GOVERNMENT. The government of this project is vested in the Project Council. A majority vote of those present at a regular meeting shall be final except for amendments.

PURPOSE. The purpose of this project shall be to provide a common cooperative base for churches, agencies and individuals within Morgan-Scott Counties as they identify and seek to meet basic human needs. This is done in the name of Jesus Christ but without imposing any doctrinal precepts on each other.

MEMBERSHIP. The membership in the corporation is open to any churches, agencies, or individuals who strive to share the common concerns and needs of the people of Morgan-Scott Counties. There are no membership fees or other requirements. The Project Council shall consist of three elected representatives of each church and their pastor as well as one designated representative of each agency participating and members at large. Those members at large shall never consist of more than one-third the membership of the council.

PERSONNEL. The personnel of this corporation shall vary as the need develops. There shall be one Executive Director who shall serve for an indefinite time as administrative officer of the Project. An Administrative Assistant shall handle routine administration and correspondence and be available to the task forces for clerical assistance. Interns and other personnel may be contracted with as the need and opportunity arises.

ORGANIZATIONAL STRUCTURE. The Project Council

shall initiate task forces to research and develop planning in specific areas of concern.

LEADERSHIP. *Officers*. As the governing board, the Project Council shall elect a Chairperson, a Vice-Chairperson, a Secretary, and a Treasurer. The pastors shall not normally be elected as officers of the corporation. The Secretary and Treasurer may be one office.

Duties. The Chairperson shall preside at all meetings of the Project Council and shall also serve as an *ex officio* member of each task force. This individual will also participate in program planning. The Vice-Chairperson shall preside at Project Council meetings in the absence of the Chairperson and shall be coordinator of the programs of the council. Therefore, the Vice-Chairperson will be a participant in the planning of each program area. The Secretary shall record the minutes of all meetings for distribution. The Secretary shall also assume the other duties as assigned by the officers of the Council. The Treasurer shall maintain the accounting system for the corporation and shall receive and disperse all funds and shall be bonded.

Elections. The officers of the corporation shall be elected annually at the second regular council meeting of each year. A nominating committee shall be formed in November of each year to nominate persons for each office. Said nominations shall be presented at the first regular meeting of the Project Council each year.

Meetings. The Project Council shall meet at least monthly to conduct all business of the corporation. Task forces and program committees shall meet separately as necessary, and they shall report at the regular council meetings. Special meetings may be called by the Chairperson or five council members at any time provided it is in writing and received by all members at least five days prior, indicating the exact business to be transacted.

Administrative Personnel. The administrative personnel shall include the Executive Director, the Associate Directors, the Administrative Assistant, the interns, and the volunteers.

The Executive Director shall be responsible for the administrative work of the corporation. As such, this person will be available to individuals, churches, each program area and the task forces as requested. The Executive Director will also serve without vote as an *ex officio* member of the Project Council. This person will actively relate to outside planning agencies, resource persons, and denominational agencies.

The Associate Directors will share the responsibilities of the Director as needed and time permits. They shall also serve as *ex officio* members of specific task forces.

The Administrative Assistant shall maintain the administrative office and handle all correspondence and administrative duties as assigned. As such, this person shall be available to the task forces and program areas for administrative assistance.

Interns shall contract with the Project Council for a specific time to serve as a consultant in their area of interest. Supervision will be the responsibility of the Executive Director in association with the Project Council.

RESOURCE ADVISORY COMMITTEE. The Resource Advisory Committee shall consist of representatives of the church denominations. This group shall meet quarterly. They shall elect their own officers. Their purpose shall be as follows: to secure support of all kinds for the ministry, to relate denominations and resource persons to the programs of the ministry, to help set goals, to enable fulfillment of mission and ministry, to act as a channel of communication.

AMENDMENTS. This constitution and by-laws may be changed by consent of majority vote of the Project Council. The proposed change must be submitted in writing to each member ten days prior to the meeting date.

GUIDELINES FOR REGIONAL CONFERENCES
OF THE DIOCESE OF ROCHESTER / Issued 1975, Revised 1976

PURPOSE OF THE REGION. The Spirit of God blesses individual parishes when there is genuine sharing among parishes. It has been this way since the beginning. An individual council may serve to clarify the manner of evangelization (Paul in Antioch for Jerusalem, Acts 15). It may provide prophetic insight or correction to other churches. It may share talents with churches who may not have the same gifts.

The Region is not only a forum for speaking and active sharing as Church, it is also a forum for listening. It is on the regional level that the Spirit can break down barriers and, in new ways, all can be one. Each Regional Conference must discover its own concrete need for this type of sharing and freely participate in regional matters.

"Various forms of the apostolate should be encouraged and in the whole Diocese, or in areas of it, the coordination and close interconnection of all apostolic works should be fostered under the direction of the Bishop. In this way, all undertakings and organizations, whether catechetical, missionary, charitable, social, family, educational, or any other program serving a pastoral goal, will be brought into harmonious action. The focus of the apostolate should be properly adopted to current needs, not only in terms of spiritual and moral conditions, but also of social, demographic and economic ones. Religious and social surveys, made through offices of pastoral sociology, contribute greatly to the effective and fruitful attainment of that goal and are cordially recommended." (*Christus Dominus*, n. 17)

RESPONSIBILITY OF THE REGION. *Extent of the Task.* The Regional Conference exists to promote shared responsibility between parish and institutions of the region, and to coordinate the various ministries and apostolates as the need arises.

Programs of formation for religion teachers, parish council members, standing committee volunteers are carried on with increasing good results in the Regions. Common exploration of community problems, ecumenical concerns, sacramental needs, and problems of evangelization are all matters for regional sharing. Just as the parish seeks to be the Body of Christ in its locale, so too, the region searches out and embodies the Spirit of Christ to the Region, becoming more and more a genuine sign of the hope and love for which the world so desperately hopes and longs.

Cooperation with Various Groups. The Regional Conference provides for opportunities for the priests to gather around matters of common concern, the formation of committees and task forces, as required, to meet the increased pastoral needs of the Region, and cooperation with diocesan bodies such as the Pastoral Council and the Pastoral Office in order to better serve the people of God.

Special Tasks. The Regional Conference, through its formal assembly meetings, and in cooperation with all the parish councils of the Region, has a special responsibility for generating leadership to serve on the Diocesan Pastoral Council. As a vital link between the parishes (and institutions) and the DPC, the Region takes particular care to insure the free and open participation of the parishes, electing three delegates to the DPC.

Furthermore, the Region brings to the DPC proposals and requests that are called to its attention by the member parishes and institutions. It provides, as well, communications back to the parishes from the DPC on a regular basis.

ORGANIZATION OF THE REGIONAL CONFERENCE.

Regional Coordinator. The Regional Coordinator is the personal representative of the Ordinary. His office is established to promote shared responsibility for the mission in the document entitled, "Office of the Regional Coordinator."

Regional Executive Committee. Functions as the Agenda Committee of the Assembly, calling for adequate homework and prior notice for proposals which the Assembly must respond to, assuring that the steps are clear as to what is being asked of the Assembly (and that it is possible for the Assembly to respond), handling the necessary internal administrative detail for the Assembly, making sure that the following have access to the agenda: parish staff and parish councils of the Region, the Bishop and Bishop's staff, the Diocesan Pastoral Council, the Priests' Council, the Sisters' Council. (Because the agenda is open, the Agenda Committee has to be rigorous in requesting that identified needs be presented to the Assembly in terms of the Assembly's stated purpose.)

Functions as the steering group for the regional standing committees, hearing their reports, offering them suggestions as to how to operate within the stated purposes. The Regional Coordinator is the chief executive officer of the Executive Committee and sees to it that the standing committees meet, have the necessary budget, materials, the necessary access to staff, [and] Bishop's staff.

Functions as the communications link between the parishes (pastors, staff and parish council) and the Region through minutes, newsletters or other appropriate channels. Communications include a record of what transpired, requests for support, implementation, agitation for the articulated needs of the Region. Some administrative staff support is needed for this function.

Duties of Members. Understand the purpose of the Assembly and standing committees. Be able to assist groups in referring a proposal, refining and preparing a proposal properly. Be able to assist committee heads to decide clearly what functions they intend to carry out.

Regional Assemblies. Exist to provide a forum in which needs are articulated and judgments made on the importance of needs that are identified.

Exist to be an energizing force, an encouraging, friendly, persuasive force to appropriate groups with the power to make effective decisions, and to execute them. These groups might include the Diocesan Pastoral Council, the Priests' Council, the Sisters' Council, the parish councils of the Region, parish staffs, various diocesan offices and agencies, and regional standing committees.

Exist to annually approve the stated objectives of the regional standing committees.

Exist to provide a forum for consultation in matters of diocesan concern, both by the Bishop and by the Diocesan Pastoral Council.

Duties of Members. Be authorized representatives from the parishes of the Region (sent by staff or council).

Study proposals on the agenda for discussion and vote, and promote the work of the Lord by voting affirmatively on the true needs and directions, and negatively on self-serving needs.

Serve when possible on standing committees or task forces set up to articulate needs, or on Executive Committee, if nominated.

Serve as an agent of persuasion and prophecy to staff or council of the parish when Assembly seeks to persuade those groups on a need that has been articulated.

Regional Standing Committees. Exist to prepare case statements on and articulation of the needs of the Region for confirmation by the Assembly; also to recommend to the Assembly the bodies that could act on these recommendations of needs to be met.

Exist to plan and execute programs of mediate ministry for the parishes of the Region. (Mediate ministry: includes training or in-service to committees, etc., so they might do their work more effectively; includes assisting those who in turn would assist the committees, etc., in doing their work better.) Both functions of the mediate ministry involve skills, background, training in methods, and probably imply the availability of professional staff to committees.

To plan and execute programs of immediate ministry for the parishes (e.g., a regional pre-cana series for the couples of several parishes).

To plan and execute programs of immediate ministry to the region (e.g., to the people in the nursing homes, to a college, to hospitals, to industry). This function involves cooperation with appropriate members of parish staffs, probably other staff support as well, to support the large numbers of volunteers that would be needed for several kinds of immediate regional ministry.

To be clear which of the above functions they are doing and which not, and to articulate this to themselves and make the appropriate internal decisions as a committee as to size of volunteer staff, extent of professional and secretarial and budget support needed, recruitment strategy, fund raising strategy.

Duties of Members. Because of the diversity of functions, the duties are difficult to spell out in any detail. In general, if you accept a position on a standing committee, do so for a specified period of time (one year, two years), stick to it, inform the chairman if you have to back out (and your reasons, if possible) and attend all meetings and work actively as a member to help the committee accomplish its purposes.

Committee Chairmen should prepare statement of objectives for the coming year for Assembly to approve, be a member of the Regional Executive Committee and report regularly on the work of the committee, request appropriate staff help with sufficient lead time to get it.

Parish Councils in Relation to the Region. Each parish council to designate and authorize representatives to the regional assembly, and actively seek to identify personnel to work on regional committees and task forces.

Each parish council should prayerfully seek out candidates capable of serving on the Diocesan Pastoral Council and put their names forward at the appropriate times. When the needs of the Church require it, the parish council should recommend proposals and policies to the DPC for consideration.

The parish council should use the opportunities offered it regionally to raise and articulate needs of the parish which the Region could address, extend to parishes and institutions of the Region services it has available and help to raise and articulate needs of the Region itself.

Because communications are important, both the council leadership and the regional leadership should make every effort to exchange news through minutes, newsletters and other vehicles available.

CONSTITUTION OF THE TOMPKINS-TIOGA REGIONAL CONFERENCE OF THE DIOCESE OF ROCHESTER / October 17, 1974

"Various forms of the apostolate should be encouraged, and in the whole diocese or in given areas of it the coordination and close interconnection of all apostolic works should be fostered under the direction of the Bishop. In this way, all undertakings and organizations, whether catechetical, missionary, charitable, social, family, educational, or any other program serving a pastoral goal, will be brought into harmonious action. At the same time, the unity of the diocese will thereby be made more evident." (*Christus Dominus*, n. 17)

NAME. This voluntary assembly is composed of the Catholic communities within the geographic area of the Tompkins-Tioga region of the Diocese of Rochester and shall be called the Tompkins-Tioga Regional Conference.

PURPOSE. The members of this regional conference have come together to cooperate with one another and to share their resources and talents to accomplish the following objectives: to increase the availability and efficiency of services for all the people within the region; to provide a representative forum for full and free discussion on matters of regional concern; to demonstrate the apostolic character of their mission to the total community; to show their mutual concern for one another; to evaluate our regional ministry and recommend priorities and suggest courses of action for improvement; to foster diocesan unity, Christian renewal, and the essential communication links among the various communities in the region; to maintain liaison with diocesan departments and provide information pertinent to pastoral renewal; and to generate, through membership, qualified candidates for the diocesan pastoral council.

ORGANIZATION. *General Assembly.* The most widely representative, and officially designated body of members having primary responsibility for the overall activities and policies of the regional conference will be called the General Assembly.

Purpose: to provide a forum for free discussion on matters of concern to regional members; to establish policies and priorities on regional matters in accordance with diocesan policies; and to receive reports and recommendations of the regional committees and act thereon, if necessary.

Membership: Each community within the region is entitled to be represented by four voting delegates. Each delegation shall consist of one priest, one sister (where applicable) and laity. Delegates shall be designated by the parish council of their community. (If no council exists they shall be designated in any manner which is representative of their community until such time as a parish council is established.) Delegates shall be named for a term of two years to begin at the October Assembly. (To establish continuity, each community shall designate two members for one year terms and two for two year terms initially.) Each participating community may designate two alternates who, with full voting privileges, participate in General Assembly meetings in place of official delegates if the need arises. The Regional Coordinator and the Associate Regional Coordinators, the Regional Representative to the Diocesan Priests' Senate, the Regional Representative to the Diocesan Sisters' Council shall be *ex officio* members with a vote.

Officers: A Chairman, Vice-Chairman, Secretary, and Treasurer shall be elected by the General Assembly from its own membership. This election shall take place at the October Assembly. The Regional Coordinator will act as, or appoint a temporary chairman for, elections. The slate of candidates shall be presented by a Nominating Committee. (For the initial meeting the existing Executive Committee shall act as the Nominating Committee.) The term of office for all officers shall be two years; no officer shall serve more than two successive terms.

Duties: Delegates shall be ready to share at the General Assembly the feelings, sentiments, and insights of their own community, and to listen with discernment as others share theirs, in order that action inspired by corporate wisdom and devoted to the common good might ensue. The Chairman, having consulted with the Executive Committee, shall determine the place, time and order of business of the General Assembly, and shall conduct its meetings. The Vice-Chairman shall act in the absence of the Chairman. The Secretary of the General Assembly shall also be the Secretary of the Executive Committee, and shall be responsible for the keeping of the minutes and their proper distribution. The Treasurer of the General Assembly shall also be the Treasurer of the Executive Committee, and shall be responsible for the accurate accounting and proper disbursement of the funds. He shall present a status report at each meeting of the General Assembly and the Executive Committee.

Meetings: The General Assembly shall meet at least two times each year, namely, in October and in May. The General Assembly will be conducted according to Robert's Rules of Order.

Standing Committees. The Standing Committees shall have the following responsibilities: to think, to conceive, to plan and to promote responsible and relevant programs designed to meet the specific needs of the various apostolates of the Church.

Purpose: To coordinate activities of the respective parish committees as they pertain to regional objectives, to communicate to proper diocesan offices the problems and needs common to parishes in the region, to provide means whereby the diocesan offices can provide services to the parishes of the region, and to provide services on a regional level which cannot as effectively be provided by individual parishes.

Membership: Each community shall appoint one official voting delegate to each standing committee. Standing Committee meetings shall be open to all members of the region who have an interest in that committee's ministry.

Officers: Voting members shall choose their own Chairman and Secretary. In the absence of officers the Regional Coordinator shall appoint a convener.

Committees: The Standing Committees shall be Education, Human Development and Liturgy. Additional committees as needed may be appointed by the Executive Committee or the General Assembly.

Executive Committee. The Executive Committee shall administer, manage and coordinate the operations of the region and the regional committees.

Purpose: to administer regional programs, to act as the Agenda Committee for the General Assembly, and to carry out policies and programs of the General Assembly.

Membership: Regional Coordinator and Associate Regional Coordinator, Chairmen of the Standing Committees, Officers of the General Assembly, and Regional Delegates to the Diocesan Pastoral Council.

Officers: The Chairman of the Executive Committee shall be the Regional Coordinator or an Associate Regional Coordinator.

Meetings: The Executive Committee should meet monthly.

AMENDMENTS. Amendments to the Constitution shall be made by a two-thirds majority of delegates present at any General Assembly. Prior notice must be given to the delegates.